# film posters of the 80s

## the essential movies of the decade

from the reel poster gallery collection

edited by tony nourmand and graham marsh

aurum press

First published in 2001 by
Aurum Press Limited
25 Bedford Avenue
London WC1B 3AT

A catalogue record for this book is available
from the British Library.

ISBN 1 85410 803 4

Art direction and design by Graham Marsh
Page make-up by Trevor Gray
Editorial assistance by Kim Goddard

10  9  8  7  6  5  4  3  2
2005  2004

Printed in Singapore by Kyodo

## ACKNOWLEDGEMENTS

Richard & Barbara Allen
Farhad Amir Ahmadi
Martin Bridgewater
Joe Burtis
Glynn Callingham
Jose Ma. Carpio
Jamie Carter
Mr Chris
Tony Crawley
The Crew From The Island
Richard Dacre
Leslie Gardner
Intellectual Property Management Associates
Eric & Prim Jean-Baptise
Warren Knight
John & Billy Kisch
June Marsh
Hamid Joseph Nourmand
Mike & Virginia Orlando
Gabrielle Pantucci
Fariborz K. Peyman
Yasumasa Takahashi
X-Man

And special thanks to
Ellen De Wachter
Bruce Marchant

The Reel Poster Gallery
72 Westbourne Grove
London W2 5SH
Tel:  020 7727 4488
Fax: 020 7727 4499
Web Site: www.reelposter.com
Email: info@reelposter.com

**37.2 Le Matin (Betty Blue)** (1986)
French 24 × 31 in. (61 × 79 cm)
(Advance)

# contents

# from wall street to your wall

The film posters of any given period offer an unerringly accurate reflection of the tastes and aspirations of the audiences they were designed to attract. For film-makers have always been quick to seize upon the prevailing fashions and preoccupations of the times and to distil them into their purest form, and the poster artist strives, of course, to carry the process even further by capturing the magic of a movie in a single graphic image.

Certainly, a cultural critic of the future flicking through these pages would quickly recognize that they originated in the 80s, the decade of the yuppie whose sole ambition was to have a bank account as bulging as Schwarzenegger's biceps, and who spent the loot on music, fashion and the latest products of high technology, clad, for preference, in matt black. This young audience, perhaps because it spent so many hours at the computer screen trying to get rich quick, also had a strong taste for vicarious violence. Our critic might

deprecate these tastes, but he or she would have to admit that, in catering to them, the cinema enjoyed a remarkably fertile decade.

Testosterone-fuelled fantasies such as *Die Hard*, *First Blood*, *Robocop*, *Terminator* and *Top Gun* enabled a new generation of stars like Stallone, Schwarzenegger, Bruce Willis and Tom Cruise to earn a handsome return on all those hours they had invested in work-outs. The ubiquitous Steven Spielberg contributed to this genre with his *Raiders Of The Lost Ark* which, almost overnight, transformed archaeology from a dim academic discipline into a profession that was as cool as they come. The other side of the Spielberg coin glittered just as brightly in *E.T.*, which had telephone companies rubbing their hands with joy as millions got the message and phoned home.

Spielberg, like his contemporaries Scorsese and Coppola, had earned his directorial spurs in the 70s after graduating from film school. In contrast, the young meteors of the 80s – Adrian Lyne,

**Bandits** (1986)
US 41 × 27 in. (104 × 69 cm)
Art direction by Thomas Starr
Design by Dan Schuman
Illustration by John Jinks

**The Cotton Club** (1984)
US 40 × 26 in. (102 × 66 cm)
(International)
Art direction by Brian D. Fox
Design by Ron Brant
Illustration by Michael Marcus & Jim Pearsall

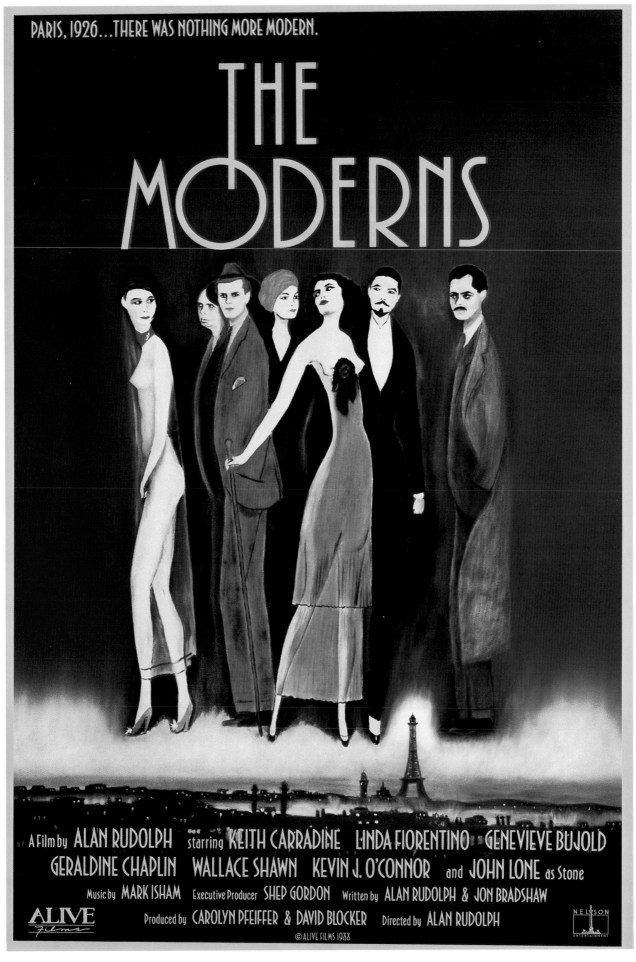

**The Moderns** (1988)
US 41 × 27 in. (104 × 69 cm)
Art direction by Rafe Blasi
Design by Randi Lynn Braun
Illustration by Keith Carradine

Alan Parker and Ridley Scott – graduated to feature films from the world of pop videos and television adverts. A progression that seems entirely logical if one recognizes that all-dancing, dolby strength musicals like *Flashdance* and *Fame* are basically videos stretched to feature length. In retrospect they may not be remembered as cinematic landmarks; but at the time they certainly did the business for aerobic classes and the manufacturers of leg-warmers.

The colossal success of *Star Wars* meant that directors were eager to take advantage of the new special effects techniques now available, and they were duly deployed, not only in the sci-fi genre, but

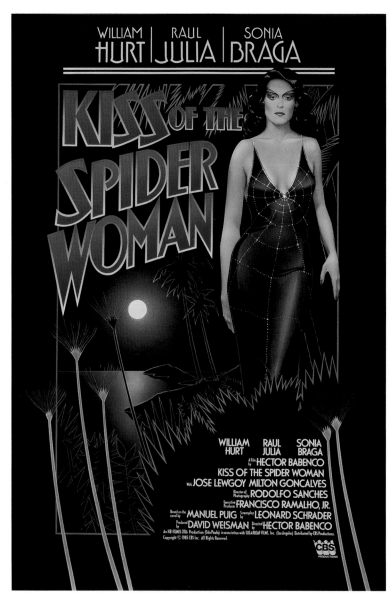

**Kiss Of The Spider Woman** (1985)
British 41 × 27 in. (104 × 69 cm)

also in movies like *Poltergeist* and *Ghostbusters*. For 80s audiences, whatever their age, really liked to be scared and Hollywood profitably stood their hair on end with *The Evil Dead*, *Friday The 13th* and *A Nightmare On Elm Street*.

For lovesick and troubled teenagers – and for twenty- and thirty-somethings who had still not cracked it – the 80s cinema prescribed appropriate therapy in the form of *The Breakfast Club*, *St Elmo's Fire*, *Diner* and *The Big Chill*; and so the careers of Demi Moore, Mickey Rourke and Jeff Goldblum were launched. America itself had a more serious trauma in its recent past – Vietnam. *Platoon*, *First Blood* and *Good Morning, Vietnam* all sought, in their different ways, to confront that scarifying legacy. More remote historical episodes provided the material for the decade's three great bio-epics: *Gandhi*, *Amadeus* and *The Last Emperor*.

There was sex, of course, served up hot and steamy in *9½ Weeks*, *American Gigolo*, *Body Heat* and *Fatal Attraction*, while comedy came slick and fast in *Caddyshack*, *Tootsie*, *Airplane* and *Ferris Bueller's Day Off*. And although the 80s were largely Hollywood-dominated, a few foreigners did get their toes in the door: the UK had a hit with *A Fish Called Wanda* and Italy scored with the enchanting *Cinema Paradiso*, one of a select few foreign films (*Betty Blue*, *Ran*, *Kagemusha*) that broke through into the international market.

As this brief summary makes clear, the 80s left a substantial cinematic legacy. And it became clear to us in the process of editing this book that the same could be said of the movie posters of the decade, many of which have become classics. A surprising number of these were created by artists and designers already distinguished in a wider field. Examples featured in these pages include work by Ralph Steadman (*Withnail and I*, page 34), Gerald Scarfe (*Pink Floyd The Wall*, page 35), Andy Warhol (*Querelle*, page 36), Jean Michel Folon (*The Purple Rose Of Cairo*, page 63), John Alvin (*Blade Runner*, page 95), Richard Amsel (*Raiders Of The Lost Ark*, page 105) and the photography by Herb Ritts for *Moonstruck* (page 83).

Other enduring 80s images are the posters for *E.T.* (page 9), *The Shining* (page 32), *The Big Blue* (page 38), *The Blues Brothers* (back cover) and *Scarface* (page 121); and anyone who was a student in those years would surely have pinned to their walls some or all of the following: *Blue Velvet* (page 58), *Down By Law* (page 56), *Drugstore Cowboy* (page 61) or *Brazil* (page 96), all of which have subsequently become cult classics. Indeed, although the 80s ended little more than ten years ago, many of the posters we have chosen for inclusion in this book have already established their right to be collected and displayed alongside the very best posters from earlier years.

**TONY NOURMAND AND GRAHAM MARSH**

**Manhunter** (1986)
US 41 × 27 in. (104 × 69 cm)

It's just you and me now, sport...

MANHUNTER

DE LAURENTIIS ENTERTAINMENT GROUP Presents

A RICHARD ROTH Production A MICHAEL MANN Film "MANHUNTER" WILLIAM PETERSEN KIM GREIST JOAN ALLEN BRIAN COX DENNIS FARINA STEPHEN LANG and TOM NOONAN Edited by DOV HOENIG Production Designer MEL BOURNE Director of Photography DANTE SPINOTTI Executive Producer BERNARD WILLIAMS Based on the Book "Red Dragon" by THOMAS HARRIS Screenplay by MICHAEL MANN Produced by RICHARD ROTH Directed by MICHAEL MANN

READ THE BANTAM BOOK

DOLBY STEREO IN SELECTED THEATRES

Original Motion Picture Soundtrack album on MCA RECORDS and Cassettes

RESTRICTED UNDER 17 REQUIRES ACCOMPANYING PARENT OR ADULT GUARDIAN

A DEG RELEASE DE LAURENTIIS ENTERTAINMENT GROUP Printed in U.S.A.

**Stand by Me** (1986)
US 41 × 27 in. (104 × 69 cm)

**E.T. The Extra-Terrestrial** (1982)
US 41 × 27 in. (104 × 69 cm)
(Withdrawn)
Photo by Steven Spielberg
Illustration by Drew Struzan

**Rain Man** (1988)
US 41 × 27 in. (104 × 69 cm)
Art direction by Barry Levinson & John Alvin
Design by Anthony Goldschmidt
Photo by Stephen Vaughn

**Local Hero** (1983)
US 41 × 27 in. (104 × 69 cm)

**St Elmo's Fire** (1985)
US 41 × 27 in. (104 × 69 cm)

**The Breakfast Club** (1985)
US 41 × 27 in. (104 × 69 cm)

# THEY ONLY MET ONCE, BUT IT CHANGED THEIR LIVES FOREVER.

They were five total strangers, with nothing in common,
meeting for the first time.
A brain, a beauty, a jock, a rebel and a recluse.

Before the day was over, they broke the rules.
Bared their souls.
And touched each other in a way
they never dreamed possible.

# THE BREAKFAST CLUB

A JOHN HUGHES Film · An A&M FILMS/CHANNEL Production "THE BREAKFAST CLUB"
Starring EMILIO ESTEVEZ · PAUL GLEASON · ANTHONY MICHAEL HALL · JUDD NELSON · MOLLY RINGWALD · ALLY SHEEDY
Written and Directed by JOHN HUGHES Editor DEDE ALLEN A.C.E. Music Composed by KEITH FORSEY Co-Producer MICHELLE MANNING Executive Producers GIL FRIESEN and ANDREW MEYER
Produced by NED TANEN and JOHN HUGHES A UNIVERSAL PICTURE
Copyright © 1984 by Universal City Studios, Inc.
Soundtrack available on A&M Records and Cassettes

**R** RESTRICTED
UNDER 17 REQUIRES ACCOMPANYING
PARENT OR ADULT GUARDIAN

Printed in U.S.A.

N.S.S. #850002

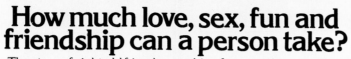

**The Big Chill** (1983)
US 41 × 27 in. (104 × 69 cm)

**Diner** (1982)
US 41 × 27 in. (104 × 69 cm)
Art by Garnett

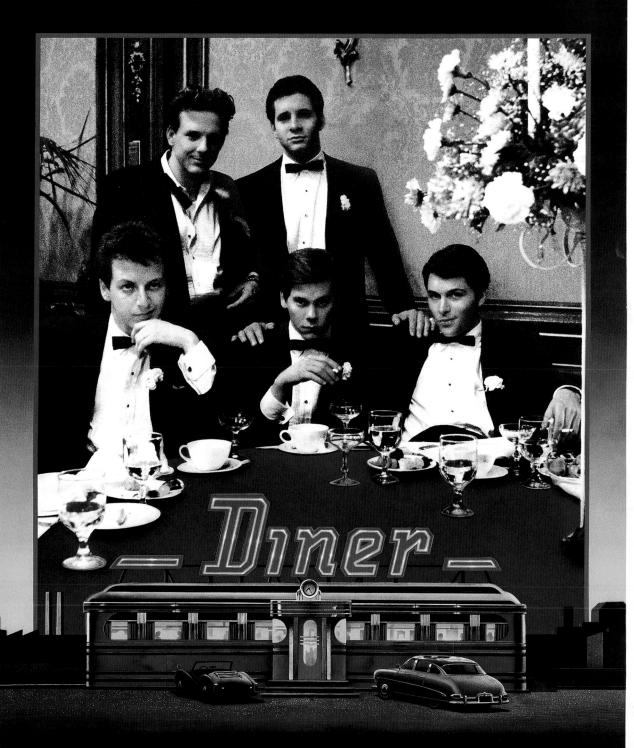

**Suddenly, life was more than french fries, gravy and girls.**

METRO-GOLDWYN-MAYER Presents
A JERRY WEINTRAUB PRODUCTION
"DINER"
STEVE GUTTENBERG · DANIEL STERN · MICKEY ROURKE · KEVIN BACON · TIMOTHY DALY
ELLEN BARKIN   Executive Producer MARK JOHNSON   Produced by JERRY WEINTRAUB
Written and Directed by BARRY LEVINSON   METROCOLOR®   Released thru MGM/United Artists Distribution and Marketing

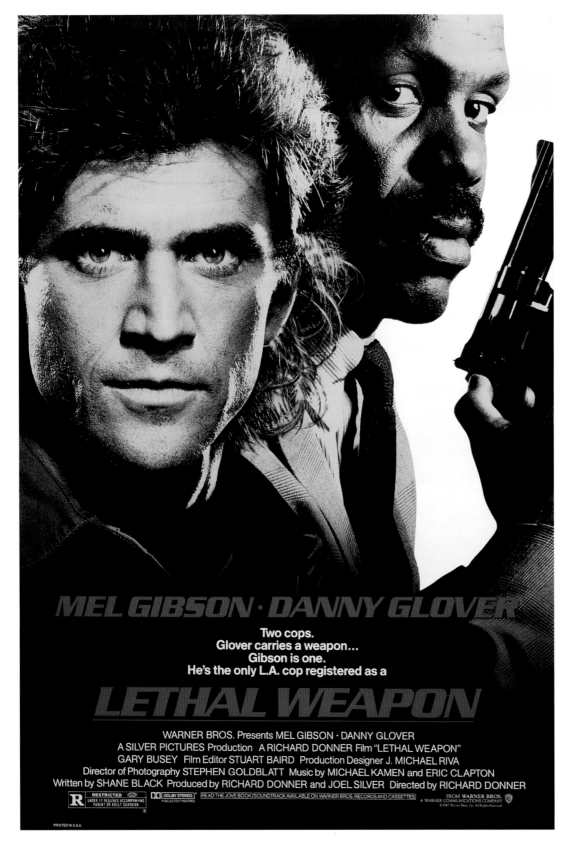

**Lethal Weapon** (1987)
US 41 × 27 in. (104 × 69 cm)
Art direction & design by Jeffrey Bacon
& David Rene
Photo by Aaron Rapoport

Twelve terrorists. One cop.
The odds are against John McClane…
That's just the way he likes it.

BRUCE WILLIS
DIE HARD

TWENTIETH CENTURY FOX Presents A GORDON COMPANY/SILVER PICTURES Production A JOHN McTIERNAN Film BRUCE WILLIS DIE HARD
ALAN RICKMAN ALEXANDER GODUNOV BONNIE BEDELIA Music by MICHAEL KAMEN Visual Effects Produced by RICHARD EDLUND Film Editors FRANK J. URIOSTE, A.C.E.
and JOHN F. LINK Production Designer JACKSON DeGOVIA Director of Photography JAN De BONT Executive Producer CHARLES GORDON Screenplay By JEB STUART and STEVEN E. de SOUZA
Based on the novel by RODERICK THORP Produced by LAWRENCE GORDON and JOEL SILVER Directed by JOHN McTIERNAN Read The Fawcett Paperback

Color by DeLuxe®

COMING THIS JULY

18

**Beverly Hills Cop** (1984)
US 41 × 27 in. (104 × 69 cm)

He's been chased, thrown through a window, and arrested.
Eddie Murphy is a Detroit cop on vacation in Beverly Hills.

# BEVERLY HILLS
*Cop*

PARAMOUNT PICTURES PRESENTS A DON SIMPSON/JERRY BRUCKHEIMER PRODUCTION IN ASSOCIATION WITH EDDIE MURPHY PRODUCTIONS · A MARTIN BREST FILM
EDDIE MURPHY · BEVERLY HILLS COP · MUSIC BY HAROLD FALTERMEYER · SCREENPLAY BY DANIEL PETRIE, JR. · STORY BY DANILO BACH AND DANIEL PETRIE, JR.
PRODUCED BY DON SIMPSON AND JERRY BRUCKHEIMER · DIRECTED BY MARTIN BREST · MOTION PICTURE SOUNDTRACK ALBUM ON MCA RECORDS AND TAPES

840117
BEVERLY HILLS COP

**Sono Otoko, Kyobo Ni Tsuki (Violent Cop)** (1989)
Japanese 30 × 20 in. (76 × 51 cm)

**Robocop** (1987)
US 41 × 27 in. (104 × 69 cm)
Art direction by Brian D. Fox
Design by Robert Biro
Photo by Deana Newcomb
Illustration by Mike Byron

**The Terminator** (1984)
US 41 × 27 in. (104 × 69 cm)

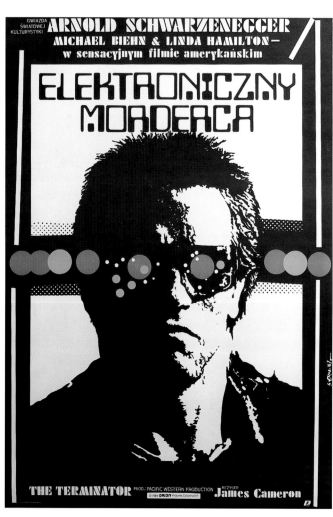

**The Terminator (Elektroniczny Morderca)** (1984)
Polish 33 × 23 in. (84 × 58 cm)
Art by Jakub Erol

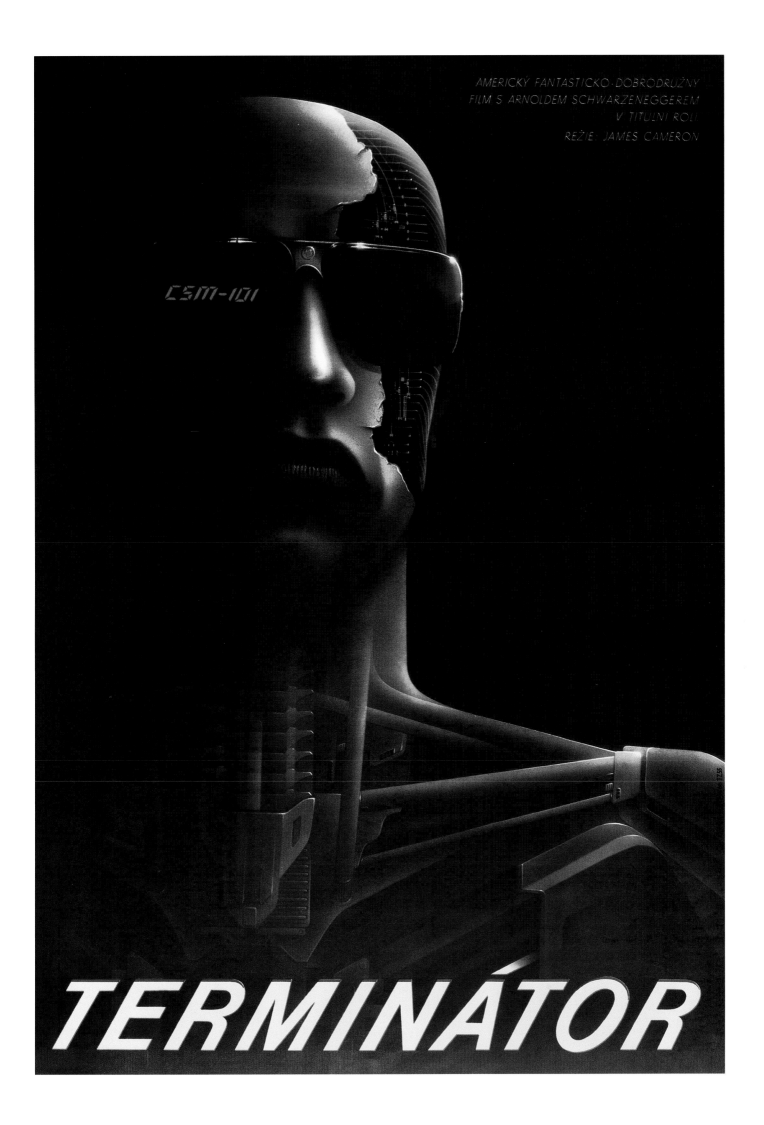

24

**Return Of The Jedi**
**(Original Title 'Revenge Of The Jedi')** (1982)
US 41 × 27 in. (104 × 69 cm)
(Second Advance)
Art by Drew Struzan

**Return Of The Jedi** (1983)
Polish 38 × 27 in. (97 × 69 cm)
(Style B)
Art by W. Dybowski

**film produkcji amerykańskiej**

**POWRÓT**

**JEDI**

REŻYSERIA:
**RICHARD MAQUAND**
W ROLACH GŁÓWNYCH:
**mark hamill · harison ford · carrie fisher**
PRODUKCJA: A LUCASFILM LTD. PRODUCTION
20TH CENTURY-FOX, 1983

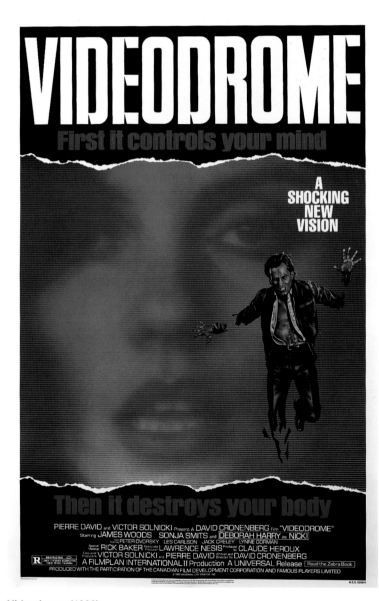

**Videodrome** (1982)
US 41 × 27 in. (104 × 69 cm)

**Dead Ringers** (1988)
US 41 × 27 in. (104 × 69 cm)
Art direction & design by Nathan Grant

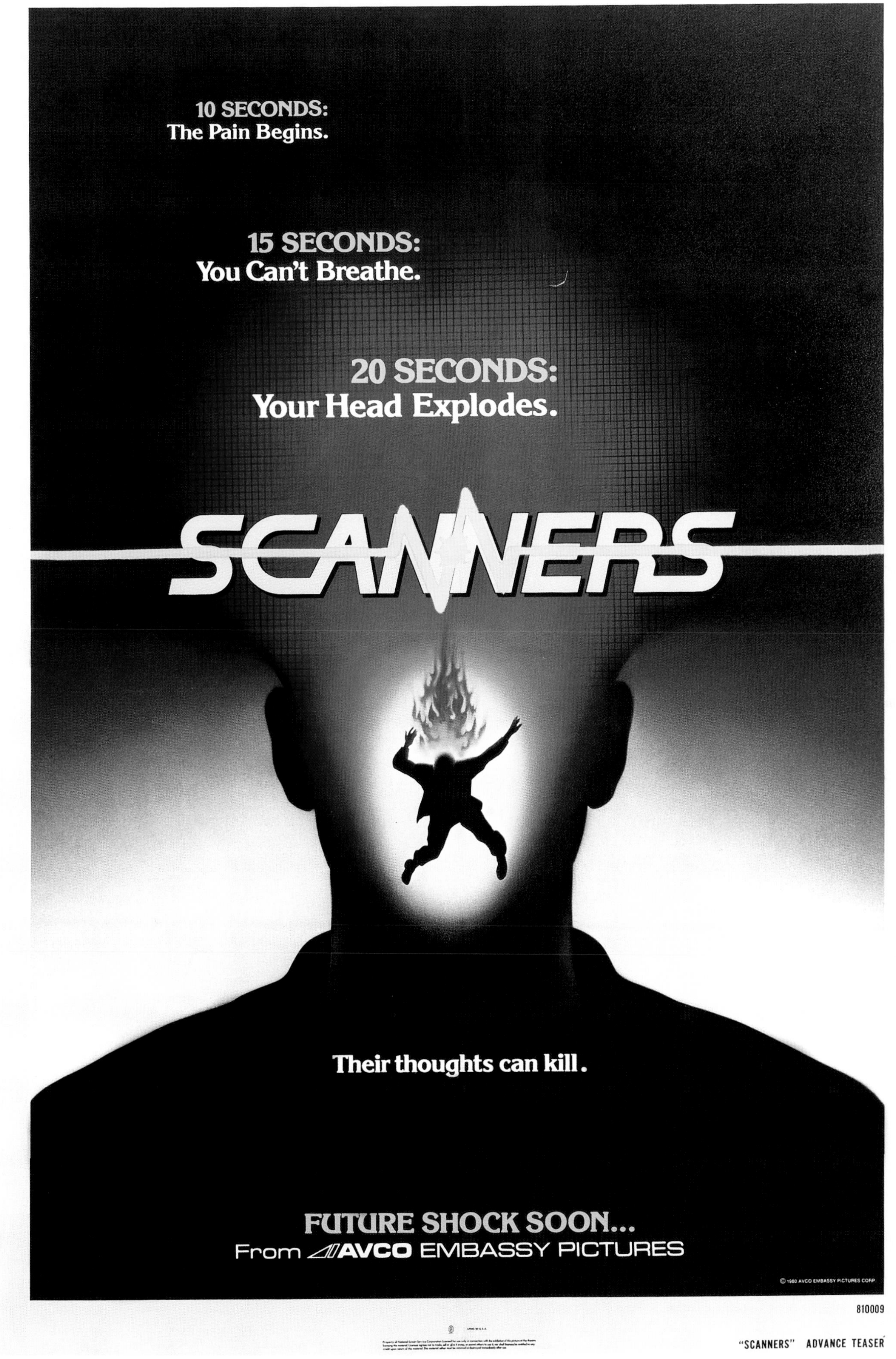

10 SECONDS:
The Pain Begins.
15 SECONDS:
You Can't Breathe.
20 SECONDS:
Your Head Explodes.
SCANNERS
Their thoughts can kill.
FUTURE SHOCK SOON...
From AVCO EMBASSY PICTURES
© 1980 AVCO EMBASSY PICTURES CORP.
810009
"SCANNERS" ADVANCE TEASER

**A Nightmare On Elm Street** (1984)
US 41 × 27 in. (104 × 69 cm)

**The Evil Dead** (1983)
US 41 × 27 in. (104 × 69 cm)

They were warned…They are doomed…
And on Friday the 13th, nothing will save them.

# FRIDAY THE 13TH

A 24 hour nightmare of terror.

PARAMOUNT PICTURES PRESENTS FRIDAY THE 13TH A SEAN S. CUNNINGHAM FILM STARRING BETSY PALMER ADRIENNE KING HARRY CROSBY LAURIE BARTRAM MARK NELSON JEANNINE TAYLOR ROBBI MORGAN KEVIN BACON DIRECTOR OF PHOTOGRAPHY BARRY ABRAMS MUSIC BY HARRY MANFREDINI ASSOCIATE PRODUCER STEPHEN MINER EXECUTIVE PRODUCER ALVIN GEILER WRITTEN BY VICTOR MILLER PRODUCED AND DIRECTED BY SEAN S. CUNNINGHAM A GEORGETOWN PRODUCTIONS INC. PRODUCTION

A PARAMOUNT RELEASE

**R** RESTRICTED
UNDER 17 REQUIRES ACCOMPANYING
PARENT OR ADULT GUARDIAN

800073

Friday the 13th

**An American Werewolf In London** (1981)
US 41 × 27 in. (104 × 69 cm)
(International)

**Escape From New York** (1981)
US 41 × 27 in. (104 × 69 cm)
Art direction by David Reneric
Illustration by Barry Jackson

**The tide of terro**

**THE**

STARRING
A STANLEY KUBRICK FILM JACK NICHOLS
BASED ON THE NOVEL BY          SCREENPLAY BY
STEPHEN KING STANLEY KUBRICK &

**The Shining** (1980)
British 30 × 40 in. (76 × 102 cm)

# hat swept America IS HERE

# ...HiNiNG x

SHELLEY DUVALL "THE SHINING" WITH SCATMAN CROTHERS    DANNY LLOYD

PRODUCED AND DIRECTED BY    EXECUTIVE PRODUCER    PRODUCED IN ASSOCIATION WITH
E JOHNSON    STANLEY KUBRICK    JAN HARLAN    THE PRODUCER CIRCLE CO.

**Withnail And I** (1987)
British 30 × 40 in. (76 × 102 cm)
Art by Ralph Steadman

**Pink Floyd The Wall** (1982)
US 41 × 27 in. (104 × 69 cm)
Art by Gerald Scarfe

**Querelle** (1982)
German 33 × 23 in. (84 × 58 cm)
(Withdrawn)
Art by Andy Warhol

**Sid And Nancy** (1986)
British 41 × 27 in. (104 × 69 cm)

A  FILM  BY  ALEX  COX  ■  DIRECTOR  OF  REPO  MAN

# SID & NANCY

EMBASSY HOME ENTERTAINMENT presents A ZENITH PRODUCTION in association with INITIAL PICTURES A film by ALEX COX

## ■ GARY OLDMAN ■ CHLOE WEBB ■ in SID AND NANCY ■

Director of Photography ROGER DEAKINS    Editor DAVID MARTIN ■ Music JOE STRUMMER, PRAY FOR RAIN AND THE POGUES
■ Co-Producer PETER McCARTHY ■ Written by ALEX COX & ABBE WOOL ■ Producer ERIC FELLNER ■ Director ALEX COX ■

Novelisation available by METHUEN Screenplay Publication by FABER & FABER    Original Motion Picture Soundtrack Album on MCA Records and Cassettes  MCA RECORDS  [ ] DOLBY STEREO  A PALACE PICTURES RELEASE

# LOVE KILLS

**The Big Blue** (1988)
US 41 × 27 in. (104 × 69 cm)

**Diva** (1981)
British 41 × 27 in. (104 × 69 cm)

Comedy, Romance and Murder

Irène Silberman Presents

.DIVA.

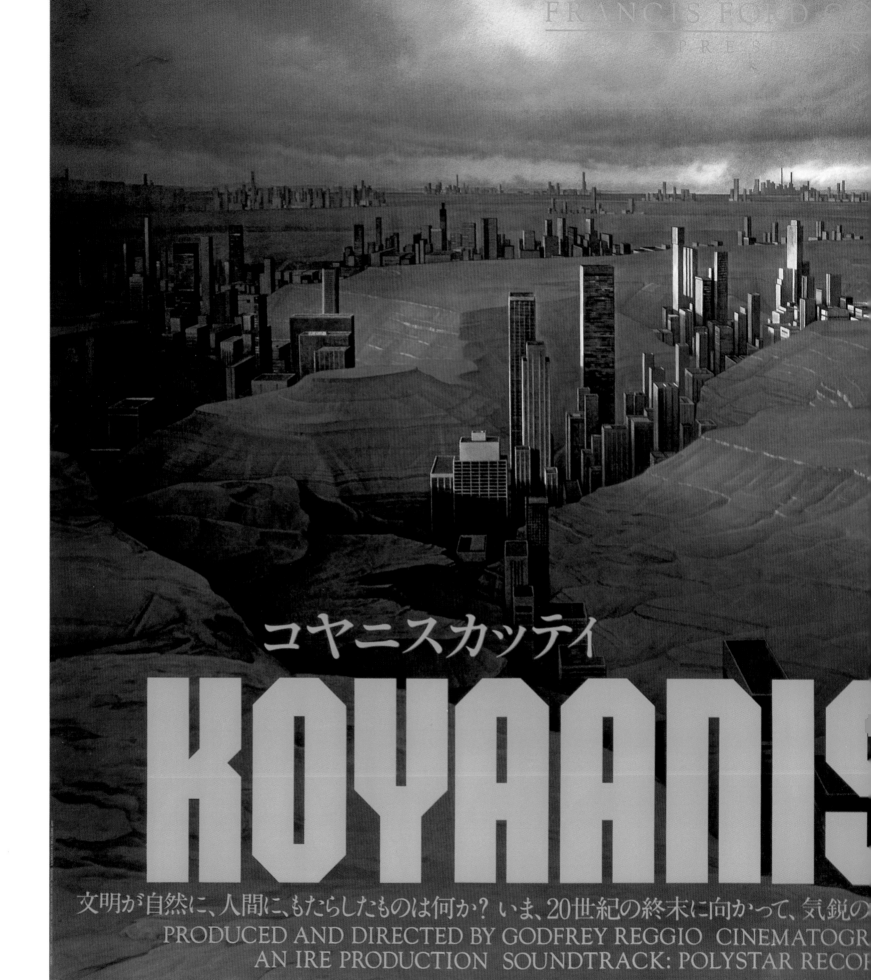

**Koyaanisqatsi** (1983)
Japanese 41 × 57 in. (104 × 145 cm)
Art by Haruo Takino
Design by Eiko Ishioka

**Wings Of Desire** (1988)
US 41 × 27 in. (104 × 69 cm)

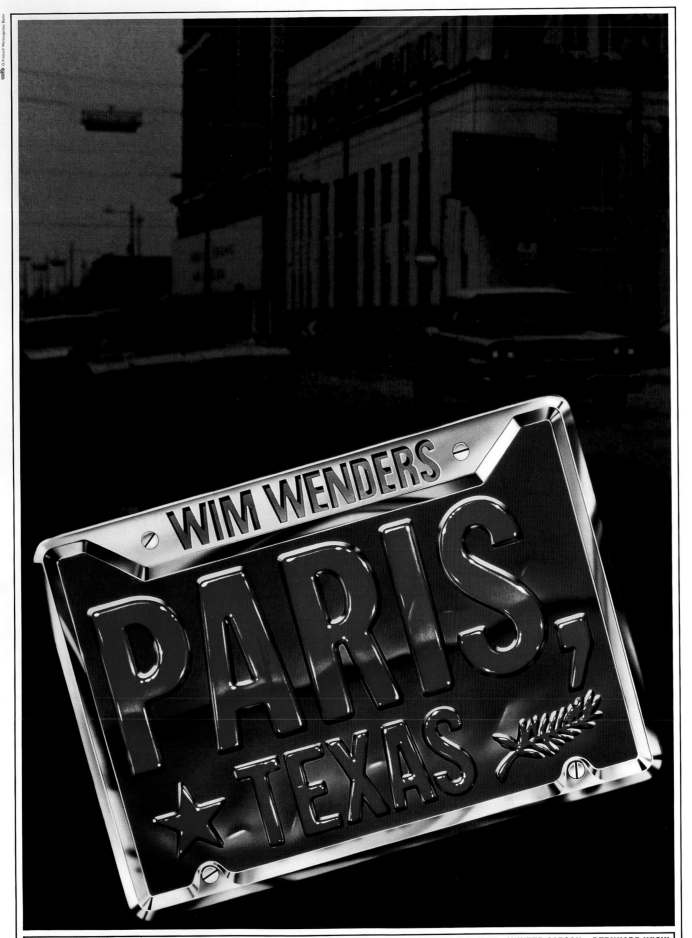

„PARIS, TEXAS" MIT HARRY DEAN STANTON · NASTASSJA KINSKI · DEAN STOCKWELL · AURORE CLEMENT · HUNTER CARSON · BERNHARD WICKI

KAMERA: ROBBY MÜLLER · AUSSTATTUNG: KATE ALTMANN · SCHNITT: PETER PRZYGODDA · MUSIK: RY COODER · PRODUZENT: CHRIS SIEVERNICH

DREHBUCH: SAM SHEPARD · BEARBEITUNG: L. M. KIT CARSON · HERSTELLUNGSLEITUNG: DON GUEST · REGIE: WIM WENDERS im Verleih der TOBIS Filmkunst

EINE DEUTSCH-FRANZÖSISCHE CO-PRODUKTION · ROAD MOVIES FILMPRODUKTION GMBH, BERLIN, UND ARGOS FILMS, PARIS · IN ZUSAMMENARBEIT MIT WESTDEUTSCHER RUNDFUNK KÖLN · CHANNEL 4, LONDON · PRO-JECT FILM, MÜNCHEN · © 1984 · DAS BUCH ZUM FILM VON WIM WENDERS IST IN ALLEN BUCHHANDLUNGEN ERHÄLTLICH

Kagemusha (1980)
Japanese 30 × 20 in. (76 × 51 cm)
(Special)
Art by Akira Kurosawa

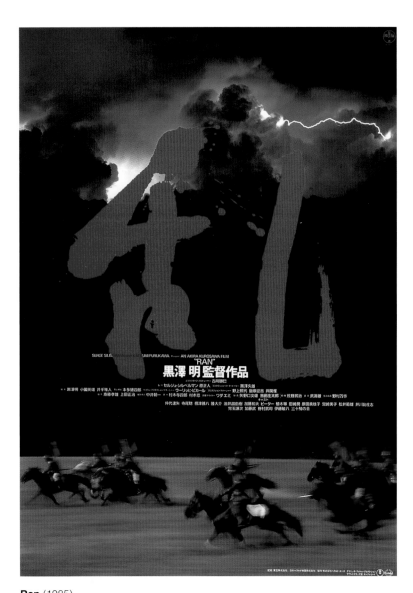

Ran (1985)
Japanese 30 × 20 in. (76 × 51 cm)
(Style A)

Ran (1985)
Japanese 30 × 20 in. (76 × 51 cm)
(Style B)

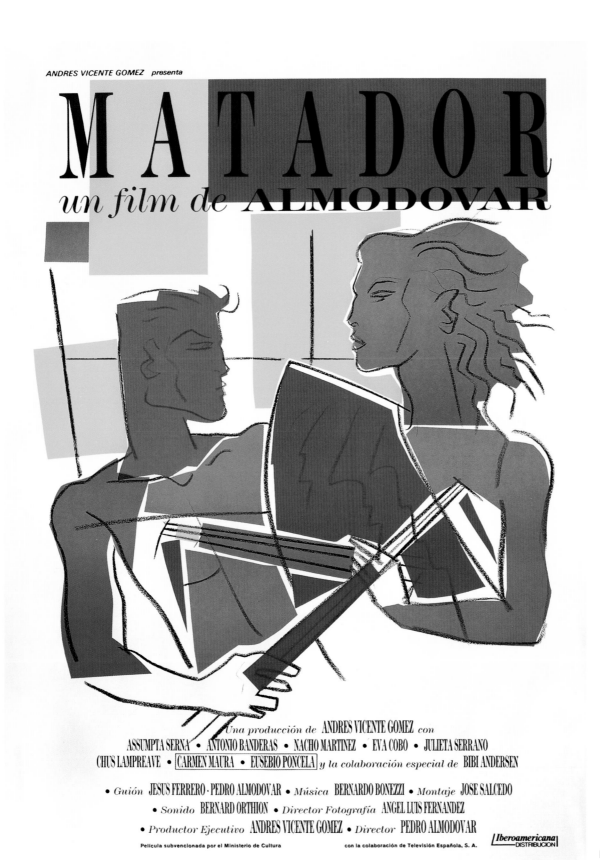

Matador (1986)
Spanish 39 × 27 in. (99 × 69 cm)

EL DESEO, S. A.    LAURENFILM    presentan

# MUJERES al borde de un ataque de NERVIOS

*un film de* **ALMODÓVAR**

**Carmen Maura • Antonio Banderas • Julieta Serrano**

María Barranco • Rossy de Palma • Guillermo Montesinos • Kiti Manver • Chus Lampreave
Yayo Calvo • Loles León • Angel de Andrés López y la colaboración de Fernando Guillén

*figurinista* José M.ª de Cossío    *sonido* Guilles Ortión    *jefa de producción* Ester García    *montaje* José Salcedo

*música* Bernardo Bonezzi    *director de fotografía* José Luis Alcaine    *productor asociado* Antonio Lloréns    *productor ejecutivo* Agustín Almodóvar

**guión y dirección Pedro Almodóvar**

Película subvencionada por el Ministerio de Cultura

**A Room With A View** (1986)
US 41 × 27 in. (104 × 69 cm)

**Nuovo Cinema Paradiso** (1989)
Italian 55 × 39 in. (140 × 99 cm)
Art by Cecchini

*Franco Cristaldi*

presenta

un film scritto e diretto da

*Giuseppe Tornatore*

una coproduzione italo·francese CRISTALDIFILM (Roma) · FILMS ARIANE (Parigi) — produzione associata RAI 3 · FORUM PICTURES SpA · T.F.1 FILM

*Titanus*
DISTRIBUZIONE

**The Sacrifice** (1986)
Russian 23 × 33 in. (58 × 84 cm)

**Nostalghia** (1983)
Russian 41 × 26 in. (104 × 66 cm)

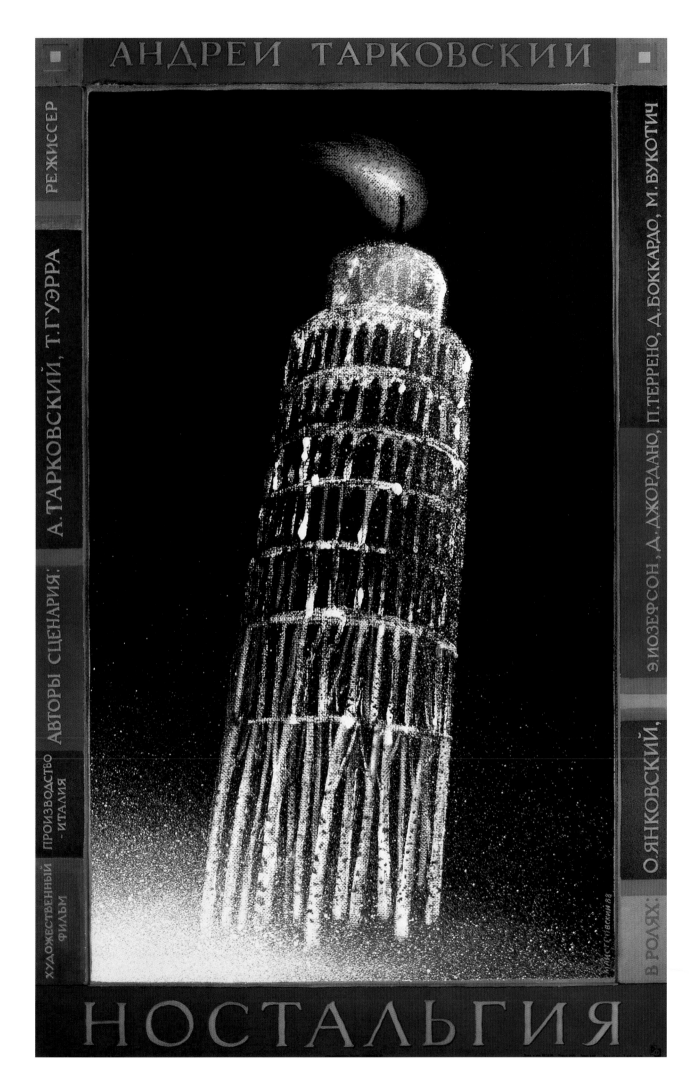

**Insignificance** (1985)
British 41 × 27 in. (104 × 69 cm)

**Sex, Lies And Videotape** (1989)
British 41 × 27 in. (104 × 69 cm)
Art direction by Mia Matson

**Stop Making Sense** (1984)
US 41 × 27 in. (104 × 69 cm)

**True Stories** (1986)
US 41 × 27 in. (104 × 69 cm)

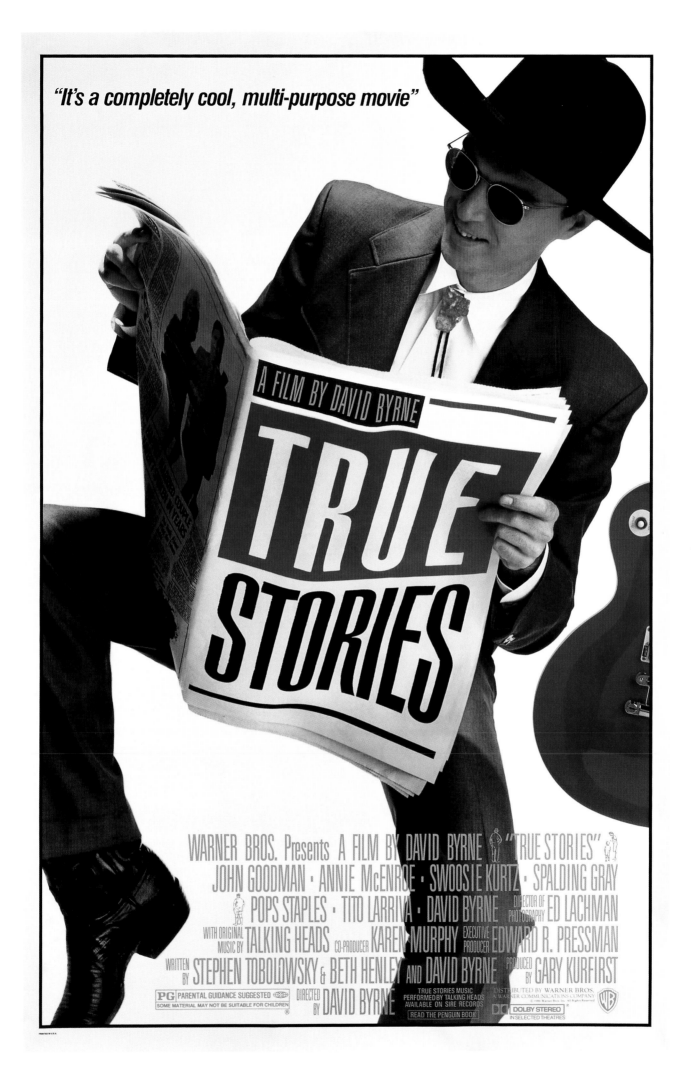

**Mystery Train** (1989)
US 41 × 27 in. (104 × 69 cm)
(Style B)
Art direction & design by Ian Gray

"Three of the damnedest performances
in an eccentric ensemble since the **Marx Brothers**."
—Andrew Sarris, Village Voice

STRANGER THAN PARADISE
A NEW AMERICAN FILM

"An enchanting film...made with heart and wit. It doesn't
feel quite like any other movie you've seen before."
Roger Ebert, Chicago Sun-Times

TOM WAITS · JOHN LURIE · ROBERTO BENIGNI
**A NEW FILM BY JIM JARMUSCH**

ISLAND PICTURES Presents A BLACK SNAKE/GROKENBERGER FILM PRODUCTION
DOWN BY LAW With TOM WAITS · JOHN LURIE · ROBERTO BENIGNI
Director of Photography ROBBY MÜLLER  Music JOHN LURIE  Songs by TOM WAITS  Editor MELODY LONDON
Co-Producers TOM ROTHMAN · JIM STARK  Executive Producers OTTO GROKENBERGER · CARY BROKAW · RUSSELL SCHWARTZ
Producer ALAN KLEINBERG  Written and Directed by JIM JARMUSCH

BEST FIRST FILM
CANNES FILM FESTIVAL 1984

THE SAMUEL GOLDWYN COMPANY PRESENTS A FILM BY JIM JARMUSCH
WITH JOHN LURIE    ESZTER BALINT    RICHARD EDSON
EXECUTIVE PRODUCER/OTTO GROKENBERGER    PRODUCER/SARA DRIVER
MUSIC/JOHN LURIE  WRITER-DIRECTOR/JIM JARMUSCH

**Down by Law** (1986)
US 41 × 27 in. (104 × 69 cm)
(Style A)

**Stranger Than Paradise** (1984)
US 41 × 27 in. (104 × 69 cm)

"...MYSTERY TRAIN is both brilliantly funny and subtle.
...MYSTERY TRAIN is thoroughly satisfying, a delight.
...MYSTERY TRAIN, an enchanting new comedy by Jim Jarmusch."
—Vincent Canby, NEW YORK TIMES

JVC PRESENTS A MYSTERY TRAIN, INC. PRODUCTION with YOUKI KUDOH
MASATOSHI NAGASE    SCREAMIN' JAY HAWKINS    CINQUÉ LEE  NICOLETTA BRASCHI
ELIZABETH BRACCO    JOE STRUMMER    RICK AVILES    STEVE BUSCEMI
and The Voice of TOM WAITS  Director of Photography ROBBY MÜLLER  Music by JOHN LURIE
Edited by MELODY LONDON  Executive Producers KUNIJIRO HIRATA and HIDEAKI SUDA
Associate Producer DEMETRA MacBRIDE  Line Producer RUDD SIMMONS  Producer JIM STARK
Written and Directed by JIM JARMUSCH
Original Soundtrack on RCA VICTOR

An ORION CLASSICS Release
© 1989 Orion Pictures Corp.

**Blue Velvet** (1986)
British 30 × 40 in. (76 × 102 cm)

*Velvet* ⑱

RTAINMENT GROUP

TS

NCH FILM

and LAURA DERN with HOPE LANGE  GEORGE DICKERSON and DEAN STOCKWELL

HAM  Music Composed and Conducted by ANGELO BADALAMENTI  Executive Producer RICHARD ROTH  Written and Directed by DAVID LYNCH

**Drugstore Cowboy** (1989)
US 41 × 27 in. (104 × 69 cm)
Art direction by Ron Michaelson
Design by Jennifer Ma Harry
Photo by Deborah Feingold

**Mala Noche (Bad Nights)** (1985)
US 47 × 34 in. (119 × 79 cm)

**Hannah And Her Sisters** (1986)
US 41 × 27 in. (104 × 69 cm)
Art direction & design by Burt Kleeger
Photo by Ryan Hamill

**Crimes And Misdemeanours** (1989)
US 41 × 27 in. (104 × 69 cm)
(Style B)

# LA ROSE POURPRE DU CAIRE

Mia **FARROW** Jeff **DANIELS** Danny **AIELLO**

UNE PRODUCTION DE Jack **ROLLINS** ET **JOFFE** MUSIQUE DE Dick **HYMAN** PRODUCTEUR ASSOCIÉ Michael **PEYSER** MONTAGE DE Susan E. **MORSE** ACE DIRECTEUR DE LA PHOTOGRAPHIE Gordon **WILLIS** ASC PRODUCTEUR EXÉCUTIF Charles H. **JOFFE** PRODUIT PAR Robert **GREENHUT** ÉCRIT ET RÉALISÉ PAR Woody **ALLEN**

**ORION** PICTURES CORPORATION

DISTRIBUÉ PAR TWENTIETH-CENTURY FOX FRANCE

**Do The Right Thing** (1989)
US 41 × 27 in. (104 × 69 cm)
Art direction & design by Art Simms
& Tom Martin
Photo by Tony Barboza
Creative direction by David Sameth

**She's Gotta Have It** (1986)
US 41 × 27 in. (104 × 69 cm)
Art by Cowell

66

**Tougher Than Leather** (1988)
US 41 × 27 in. (104 × 69 cm)

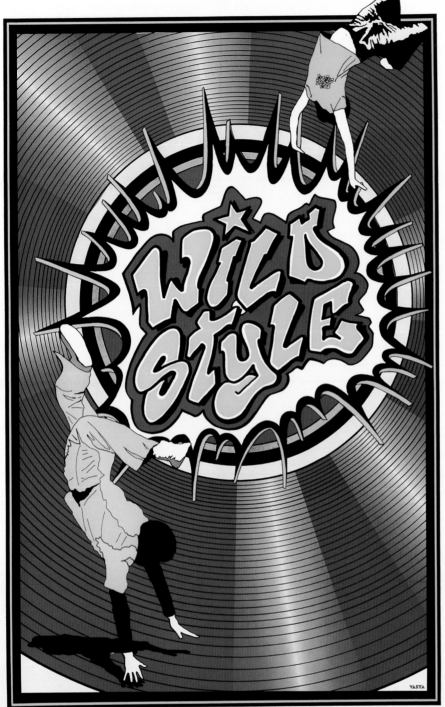

**Wild Style** (1982)
US 41 × 27 in. (104 × 69 cm)

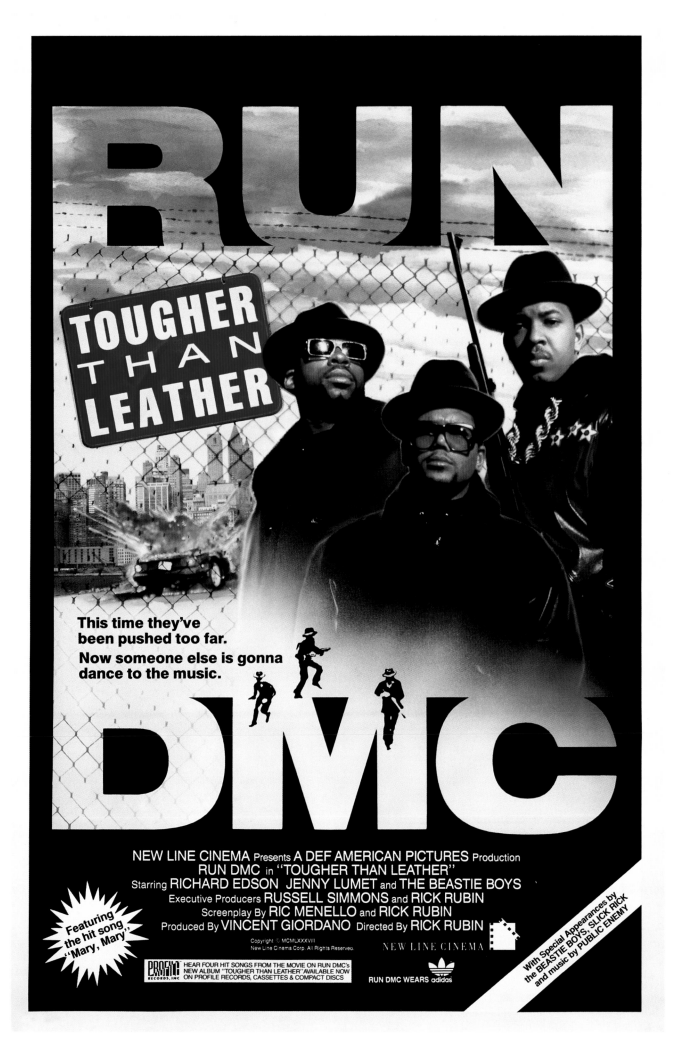

**Thelonious Monk: Straight No Chaser** (1989)
US 41 × 27 in. (104 × 69 cm)
Art direction by Bill Gold
Design by Jim Hedden

"bread, butter, and champagne"

little bear films and nan bush present

a film by
bruce weber

director of photography
jeff preiss

music by
chet baker

executive producer
nan bush

editor
angelo corrao

with

cherry vanilla
lisa marie
olga liriano
andy minsker
and
flea

let's get lost

starring
chet baker

Young, beautiful, passionate
and scandalous. She was America
in the time of "Ragtime."

DINO DE LAURENTIIS PRESENTS A MILOS FORMAN FILM

"RAGTIME" Starring JAMES CAGNEY  Music by RANDY NEWMAN  A SUNLEY PRODUCTION  Executive Producers MICHAEL HAUSMAN
and BERNARD WILLIAMS  Screenplay by MICHAEL WELLER From the Novel "Ragtime" by E.L. DOCTOROW  Produced by DINO DE LAURENTIIS
Directed by MILOS FORMAN  Read the Bantam Book  Soundtrack Album on Elektra Records and Tapes

A PARAMOUNT PICTURE

810179
"RAGTIME"

**Ragtime** (1981)
US 41 × 27 in. (104 × 69 cm)

**The Color Purple** (1985)
US 41 × 27 in. (104 × 69 cm)
Design by Anthony Goldschmidt
Illustration by John Alvin

A STEVEN SPIELBERG
FILM

# The Color Purple

Alice Walker's Pulitzer Prize Winning Story

It's about life. It's about love. It's about us.

WARNER BROS. Presents A STEVEN SPIELBERG Film THE COLOR PURPLE Starring DANNY GLOVER
ADOLPH CAESAR • MARGARET AVERY • RAE DAWN CHONG and Introducing WHOOPI GOLDBERG as Celie
Director of Photography ALLEN DAVIAU   Production Designer J. MICHAEL RIVA   Film Editor MICHAEL KAHN, A.C.E.   Music QUINCY JONES
Based upon the novel by ALICE WALKER   Screenplay by MENNO MEYJES   Executive Producers JON PETERS and PETER GUBER
Produced by STEVEN SPIELBERG • KATHLEEN KENNEDY • FRANK MARSHALL • QUINCY JONES   Directed by STEVEN SPIELBERG

72

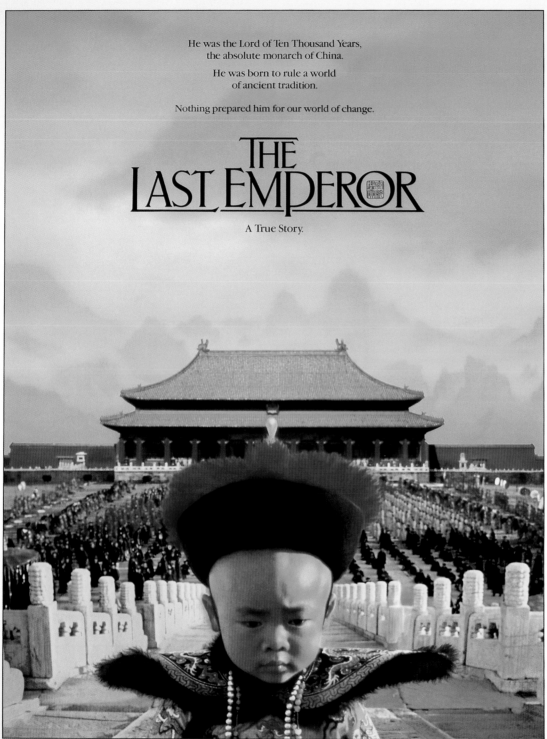

He was the Lord of Ten Thousand Years,
the absolute monarch of China.

He was born to rule a world
of ancient tradition.

Nothing prepared him for our world of change.

# THE LAST EMPEROR

A True Story.

HEMDALE FILM CORPORATION PRESENTS
A JEREMY THOMAS PRODUCTION A FILM BY BERNARDO BERTOLUCCI
JOHN LONE    JOAN CHEN
PETER O'TOOLE AS R.J.
"THE LAST EMPEROR"
YING RUOCHENG    VICTOR WONG    DENNIS DUN AND RYUICHI SAKAMOTO
ASSOCIATE PRODUCER (U.K.) JOYCE HERLIHY PRODUCTION SUPERVISOR MARIO COTONE COSTUMES JAMES ACHESON PRODUCTION DESIGNER FERDINANDO SCARFIOTTI
EDITOR GABRIELLA CRISTIANI PHOTOGRAPHY BY VITTORIO STORARO (AIC) MUSIC RYUICHI SAKAMOTO DAVID BYRNE AND CONG SU
ASSOCIATE PRODUCER FRANCO GIOVALE SCREENPLAY MARK PEPLOE WITH BERNARDO BERTOLUCCI PRODUCER JEREMY THOMAS DIRECTOR BERNARDO BERTOLUCCI

PG-13 PARENTS STRONGLY CAUTIONED   DOLBY STEREO   EASTMAN COLOR TECHNOVISION CAMERAS & LENSES TECHNICOLOR (ROME)   A COLUMBIA PICTURES RELEASE
Some Material May Be Inappropriate for Children Under 13   IN SELECTED THEATRES   SOUNDTRACK ALBUM "THE LAST EMPEROR" AVAILABLE ON VIRGIN RECORDS   © 1987 COLUMBIA PICTURES INDUSTRIES, INC. ALL RIGHTS RESERVED.   Columbia Pictures
© PRINTED IN U.S.A.   NSS 870142

**The Last Emperor** (1987)
US 41 × 27 in. (104 × 69 cm)
Art direction by Tony Seiniger
Design by Tony Seiniger & Scott Miller

**Out Of Africa** (1985)
US 41 × 27 in. (104 × 69 cm)

BASED ON A TRUE STORY.

# ROBERT REDFORD    MERYL STREEP

### A SYDNEY POLLACK Film

# OUT OF AFRICA

A MIRAGE Production "OUT OF AFRICA"

## KLAUS MARIA BRANDAUER
Co-Starring

Co-Producer **TERRY CLEGG**    Executive Producer **KIM JORGENSEN**    Associate Producers **JUDITH THURMAN** and **ANNA CATALDI**    Music by **JOHN BARRY**

Screenplay by **KURT LUEDTKE**    Produced and Directed by **SYDNEY POLLACK**

PG PARENTAL GUIDANCE SUGGESTED
SOME MATERIAL MAY NOT BE SUITABLE FOR CHILDREN

Based on the books "Out of Africa", "Shadows on the Grass" and "Letters from Africa" by Isak Dinesen; "Isak Dinesen: The Life of a Storyteller" by Judith Thurman; "Silence Will Speak" by Errol Trzebinski.

DOLBY STEREO
IN SELECTED THEATRES

A UNIVERSAL Picture
© 1984, 1985 Universal City Studios, Inc.

PRINTED IN U.S.A.

NSS #850097

**Amadeus** (1984)
US 41 × 27 in. (104 × 69 cm)
Art direction & design by Robert Faulkner
Creative direction by Mike Kaiser
Illustration by Peter Sis

**The Draughtsman's Contract** (1982)
US 41 × 27 in. (104 × 69 cm)
Art by Sparacio

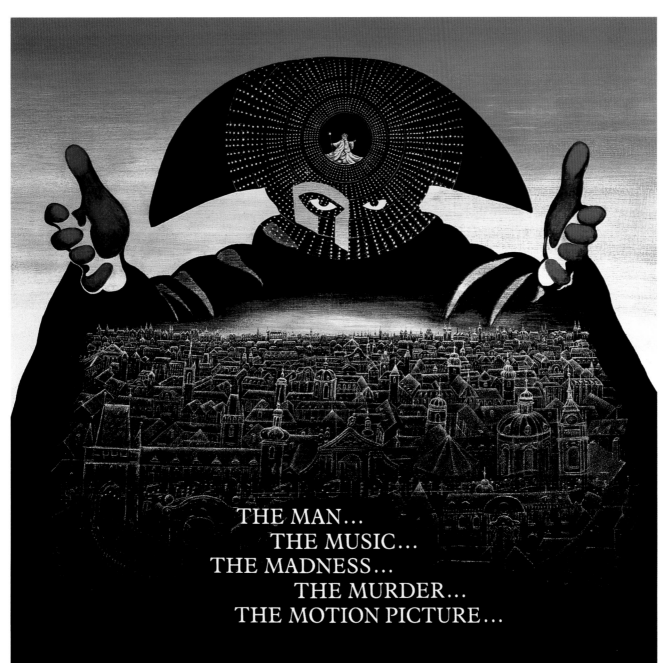

THE MAN...
THE MUSIC...
THE MADNESS...
THE MURDER...
THE MOTION PICTURE...

# AMADEUS

...EVERYTHING YOU'VE HEARD IS TRUE

The SAUL ZAENTZ Company Presents   PETER SHAFFER'S  AMADEUS  A MILOS FORMAN Film
F. MURRAY ABRAHAM      TOM HULCE      ELIZABETH BERRIDGE
with SIMON CALLOW      ROY DOTRICE      CHRISTINE EBERSOLE
JEFFREY JONES      CHARLES KAY
Executive Producers MICHAEL HAUSMAN and BERTIL OHLSSON   Director of Photography MIROSLAV ONDRICEK
Music Conducted and Supervised by NEVILLE MARRINER   Production Designer PATRIZIA VON BRANDENSTEIN   Choreographer TWYLA THARP
Screenplay and original stage play by PETER SHAFFER   Produced by SAUL ZAENTZ   Directed by MILOS FORMAN

An **ORION** PICTURES Release   70 mm DOLBY STEREO IN SELECTED THEATRES   Filmed in PANAVISION®   Prints by TECHNICOLOR®   **PG** PARENTAL GUIDANCE SUGGESTED
© 1984 THE SAUL ZAENTZ COMPANY. ALL RIGHTS RESERVED.   SOME MATERIAL MAY NOT BE SUITABLE FOR CHILDREN
PRINTED IN U.S.A.

**Chariots Of Fire** (1981)
US 41 × 27 in. (104 × 69 cm)

**Gandhi** (1982)
Polish 40 × 28 in. (102 × 71 cm)
Art by Wouman

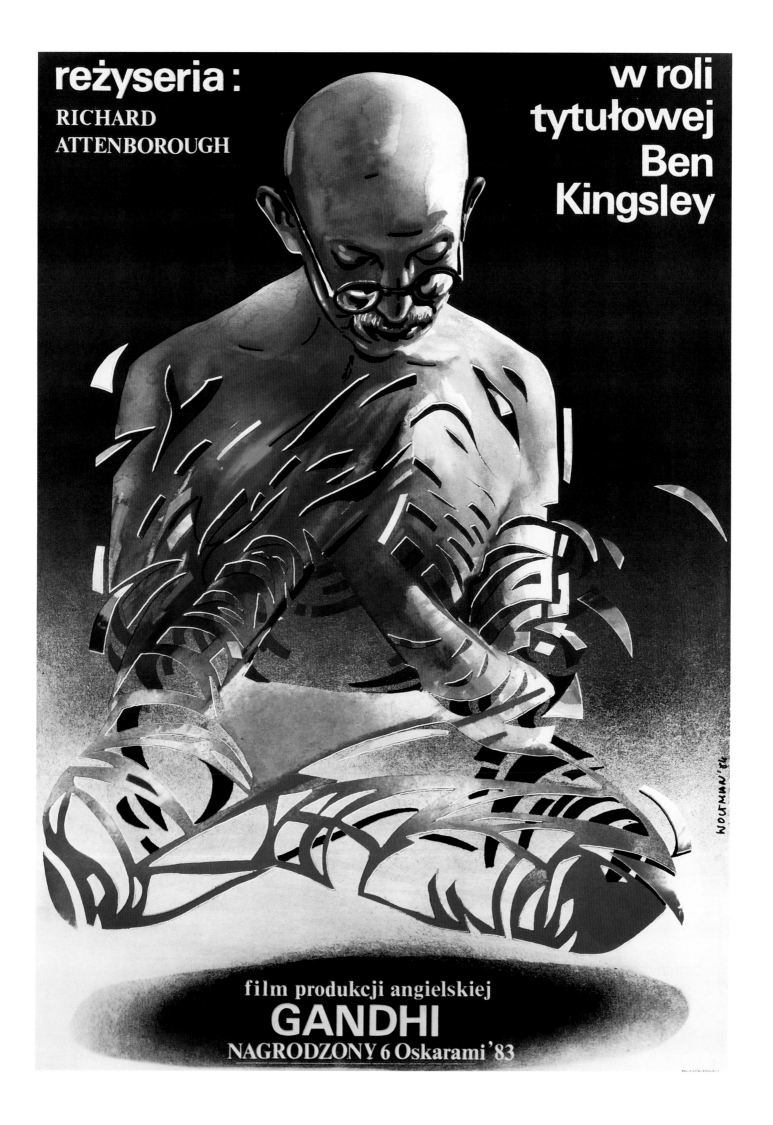

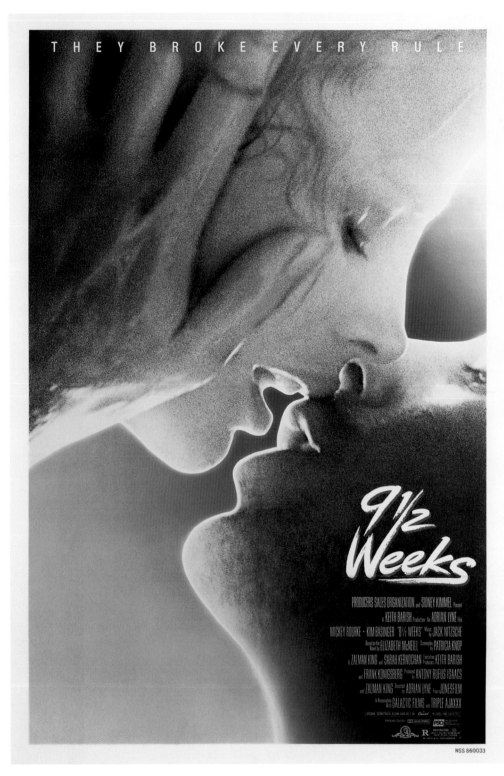

**9 ¹/₂ Weeks** (1986)
US 41 × 27 in. (104 × 69 cm)

**Fatal Attraction** (1987)
US 41 × 27 in. (104 × 69 cm)
Art direction by Peter Bemis
Design by Gina Stone
Photo by Wayne Maiser

79

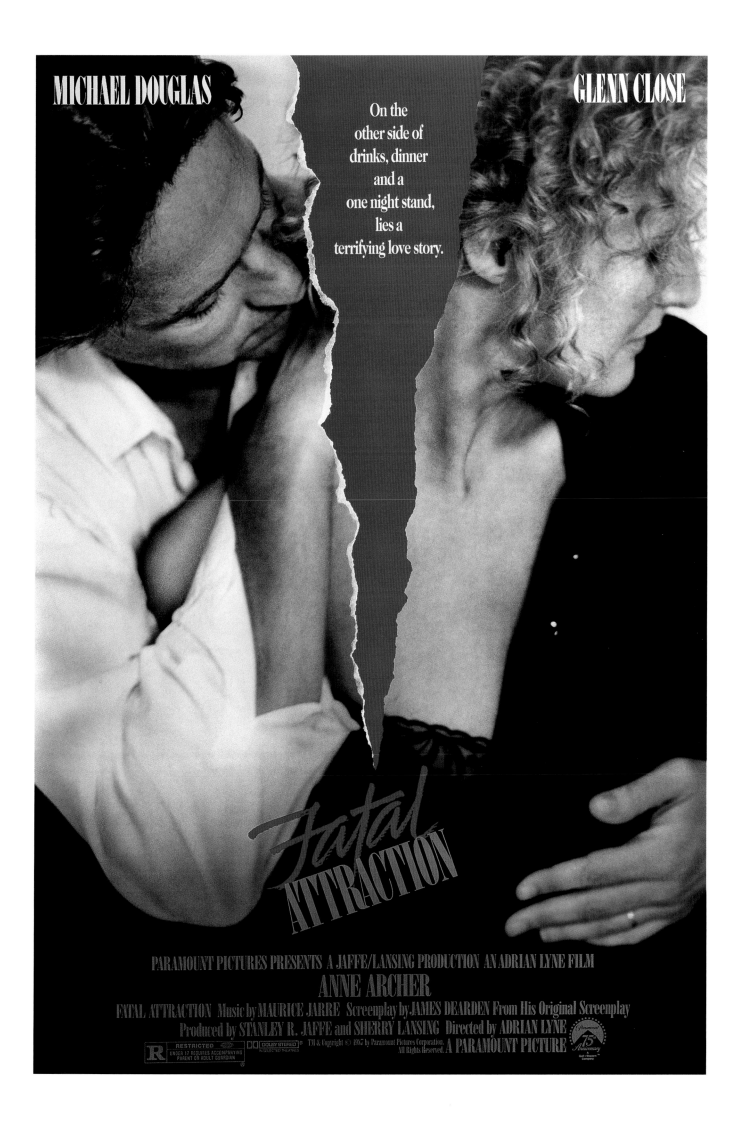

**Flashdance** (1983)
US 41 × 27 in. (104 × 69 cm)
Art direction by Tal Stubis
Design by Spiros Associates
Photo by John Shannon

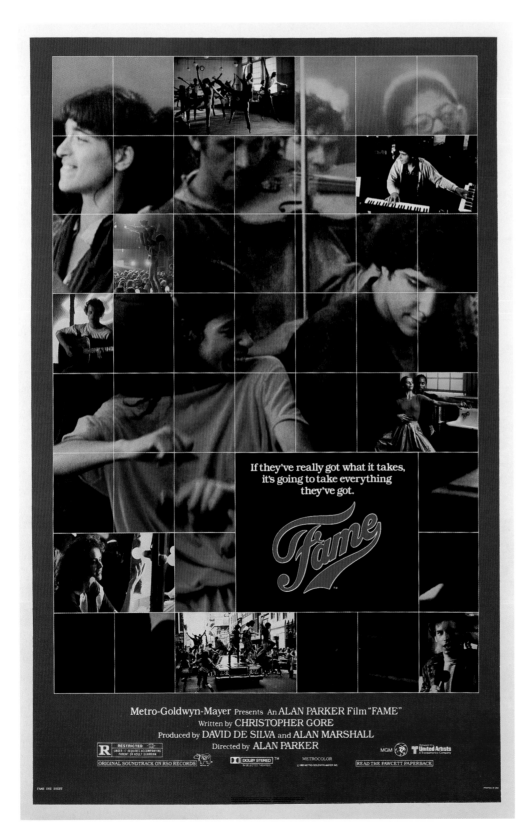

**Fame** (1980)
US 41 × 27 in. (104 × 69 cm)
Art direction by Tony Seiniger
Design by Lili Lakich

**Desperately Seeking Susan** (1985)
US 41 × 27 in. (104 × 69 cm)

**Moonstruck** (1987)
US 41 × 27 in. (104 × 69 cm)
(Style A)
Art direction by Tony Seiniger
Design by Olga Kaljakin
Photo by Herb Ritts

# MOONSTRUCK

## CHER · NICOLAS CAGE

METRO-GOLDWYN-MAYER PRESENTS A PATRICK PALMER-NORMAN JEWISON PRODUCTION

A NORMAN JEWISON FILM

"MOONSTRUCK" STARRING VINCENT GARDENIA OLYMPIA DUKAKIS AND DANNY AIELLO MUSIC COMPOSED AND ADAPTED BY DICK HYMAN

PRODUCTION DESIGNER PHILIP ROSENBERG COSTUME DESIGNER THEONI V. ALDREDGE DIRECTOR OF PHOTOGRAPHY DAVID WATKIN FILM EDITOR LOU LOMBARDO

ASSOCIATE PRODUCER BONNIE PALEF WRITTEN BY JOHN PATRICK SHANLEY PRODUCED BY PATRICK PALMER & NORMAN JEWISON

DIRECTED BY NORMAN JEWISON

**An Officer And A Gentleman** (1982)
US 41 × 27 in. (104 × 69 cm)

**American Gigolo** (1980)
US 41 × 27 in. (104 × 69 cm)

He's the highest paid lover in Beverly Hills.

He leaves women feeling more alive than they've ever felt before.

Except one.

*American Gigolo*

Paramount Pictures Presents   A Freddie Fields Production   A Film by Paul Schrader   Richard Gere in "American Gigolo"
Lauren Hutton   Executive Producer Freddie Fields   Produced by Jerry Bruckheimer   Music Composed by Giorgio Moroder
Written and Directed by Paul Schrader   Original Soundtrack Recording on Polydor Records and Tapes   A Paramount Picture

**The Verdict** (1982)
US 41 × 27 in. (104 × 69 cm)

# MICHAEL DOUGLAS   CHARLIE SHEEN   DARYL HANNAH

Every dream has a price.

AN OLIVER STONE FILM

# WALL STREET

TWENTIETH CENTURY FOX PRESENTS · AN EDWARD R. PRESSMAN PRODUCTION · AN OLIVER STONE FILM
MICHAEL DOUGLAS · CHARLIE SHEEN · DARYL HANNAH · MARTIN SHEEN · WALL STREET
HAL HOLBROOK AND TERENCE STAMP  DIRECTOR OF PHOTOGRAPHY ROBERT RICHARDSON  CO-PRODUCER A. KITMAN HO
WRITTEN BY STANLEY WEISER & OLIVER STONE  PRODUCED BY EDWARD R. PRESSMAN  DIRECTED BY OLIVER STONE

Produced in association with Amercent Films and American Entertainment Partners L.P. Distributed by Twentieth Century Fox Film Corporation  Color by Deluxe®

DOLBY STEREO
IN SELECTED THEATRES

20th CENTURY FOX

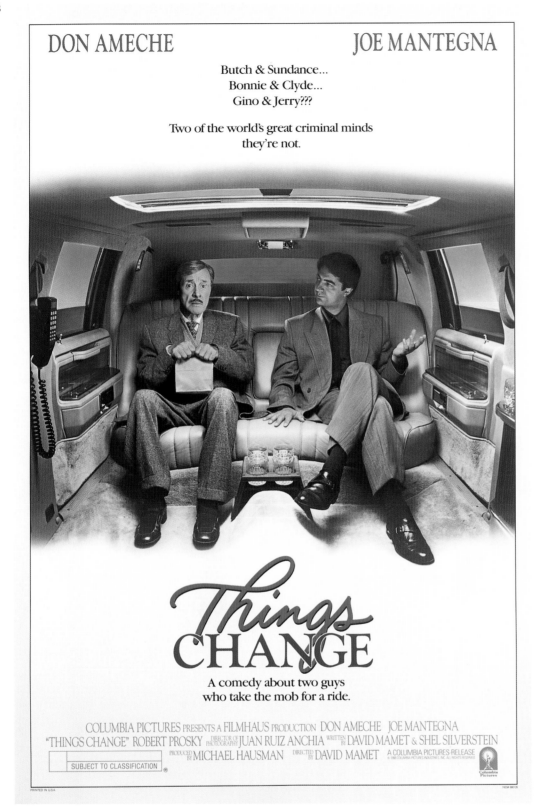

**Things Change** (1988)
US 41 × 27 in. (104 × 69 cm)

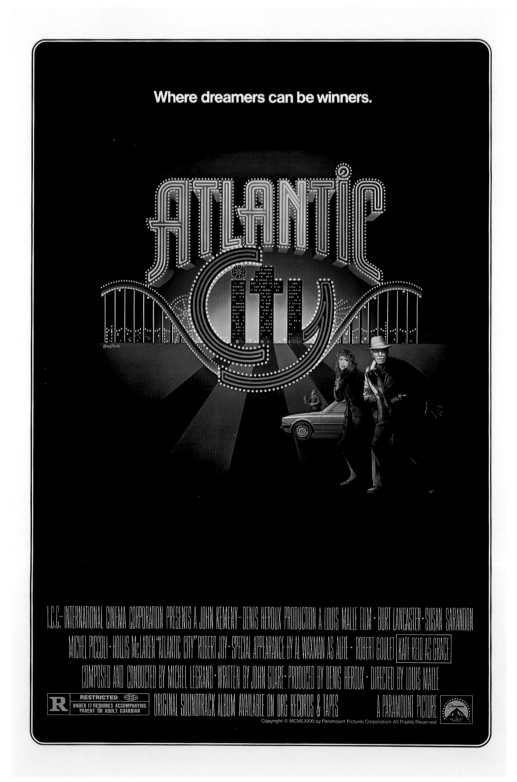

**Atlantic City** (1981)
US 41 × 27 in. (104 × 69 cm)

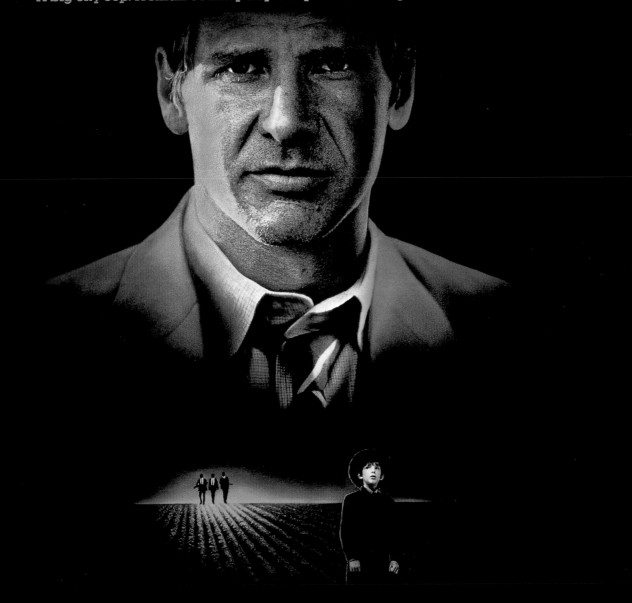

# Harrison Ford is John Book.

A big city cop. A small country boy. They have nothing in common ...but a murder.

# WITNESS

PARAMOUNT PICTURES PRESENTS AN EDWARD S. FELDMAN PRODUCTION
HARRISON FORD · WITNESS · CO-PRODUCER DAVID BOMBYK · SCREENPLAY BY
EARL W. WALLACE & WILLIAM KELLEY · STORY BY WILLIAM KELLEY AND
PAMELA WALLACE & EARL W. WALLACE · PRODUCED BY EDWARD S. FELDMAN
DIRECTED BY PETER WEIR · READ THE PAPERBACK FROM POCKET BOOKS.

A PARAMOUNT PICTURE

**Blood Simple** (1984)
US 41 × 27 in. (104 × 69 cm)

**Body Heat** (1981)
British 41 × 27 in. (104 × 69 cm)

She taught him everything she knew
– about passion and murder.

BODY
HEAT

"BODY HEAT" WILLIAM HURT  KATHLEEN TURNER
and RICHARD CRENNA  Written and Directed by LAWRENCE KASDAN
Produced by FRED T. GALLO PANAVISION® TECHNICOLOR®

A LADD COMPANY RELEASE    THRU WARNER BROS.
© 1982 The Ladd Company All Rights Reserved   A WARNER COMMUNICATIONS COMPANY

PRINTED IN ENGLAND BY W. E. BERRY LTD. BRADFORD

**Blade Runner** (1982)
US 17 × 14 in. (43 × 36 cm)

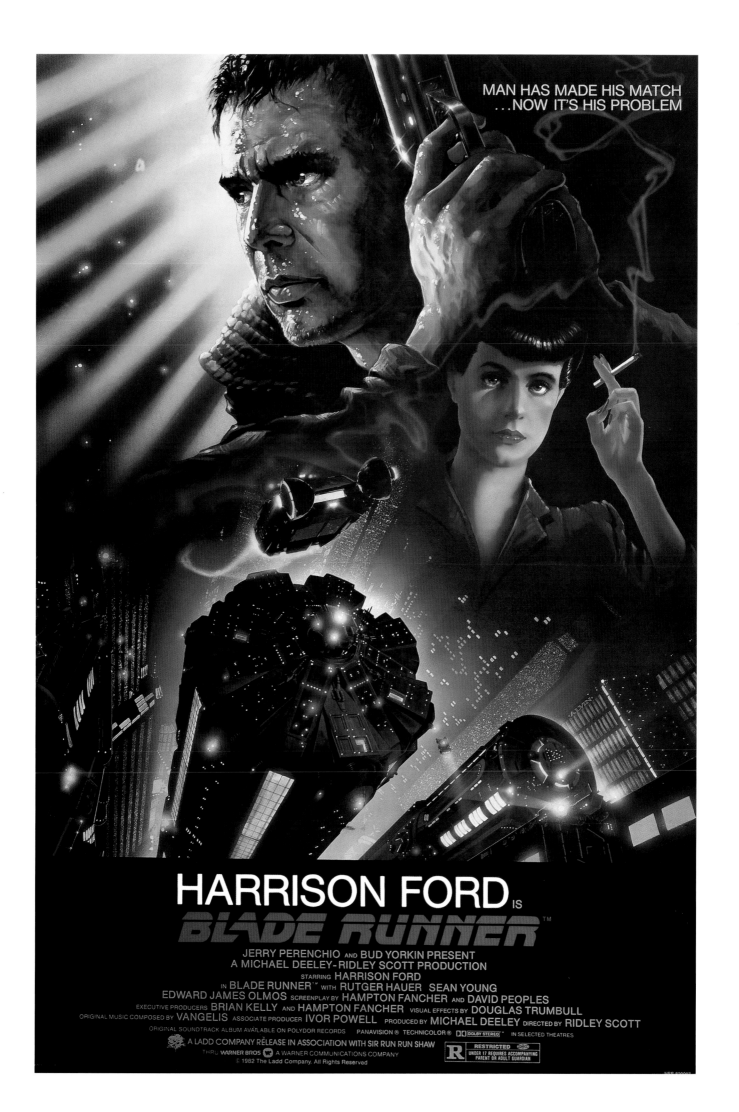

**Brazil** (1985)
British 30 × 40 in. (76 × 102 cm)
(Style B)

**Pale Rider** (1985)
US 41 × 27 in. (104 × 69 cm)
(International)
Art by C. Michael Dudash

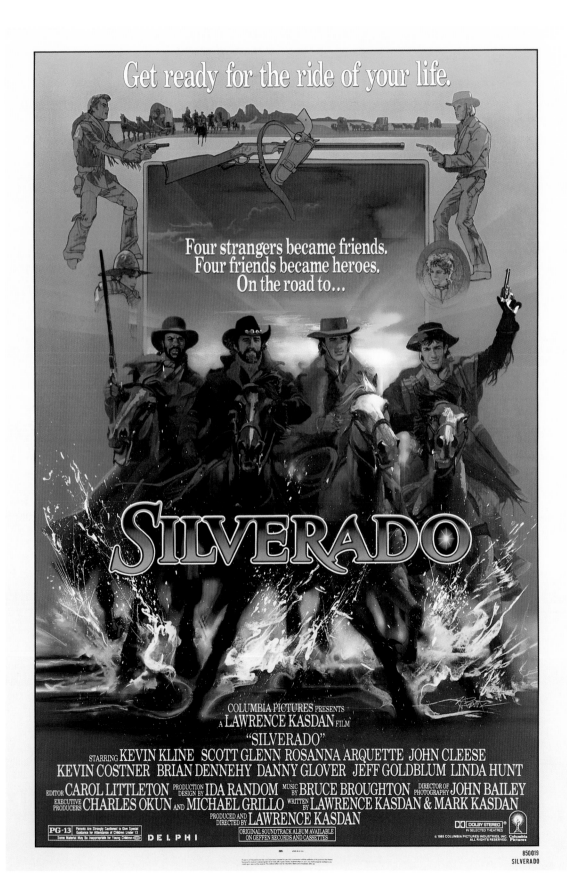

**Silverado** (1985)
US 41 × 27 in. (104 × 69 cm)
Art by Bob Peak

**Good Morning Vietnam** (1987)
US 41 × 27 in. (104 × 69 cm)
Art direction & design by Tony Stella
Photo by Bonnie Schiffman
Creative direction by Robert Jahn

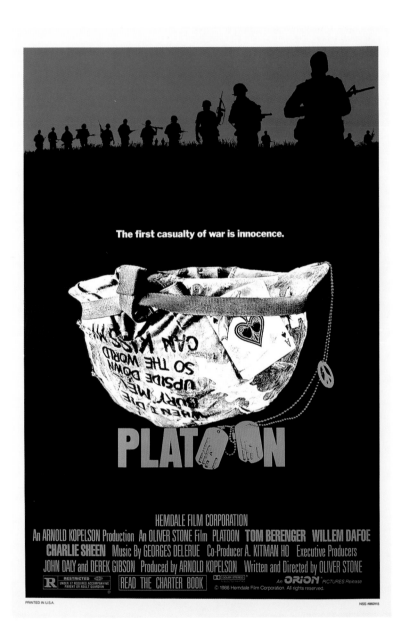

**Full Metal Jacket** (1987)
US 41 × 27 in. (104 × 69 cm)
(Advance)

**Platoon** (1986)
US 41 × 27 in. (104 × 69 cm)

# R O B I N   W I L L I A M S

In 1965, military D.J. Adrian Cronauer was sent to Vietnam to build morale.
His strategy: keep 'em laughing. His problem: staying out of trouble.

The wrong man. In the wrong place. At the right time.

A BARRY LEVINSON FILM

TOUCHSTONE PICTURES Presents in association with SILVER SCREEN PARTNERS III A ROLLINS, MORRA and BREZNER Production
A BARRY LEVINSON Film ROBIN WILLIAMS "GOOD MORNING, VIETNAM" FOREST WHITAKER Original Score by ALEX NORTH
Co-Produced by BEN MOSES Written by MITCH MARKOWITZ Produced by MARK JOHNSON & LARRY BREZNER
Directed by BARRY LEVINSON   Color by DE LUXE®   Soundtrack on A&M Records    TOUCHSTONE PICTURES
DOLBY STEREO
IN SELECTED THEATRES
© 1987 Touchstone Pictures

NSS≠ 870055

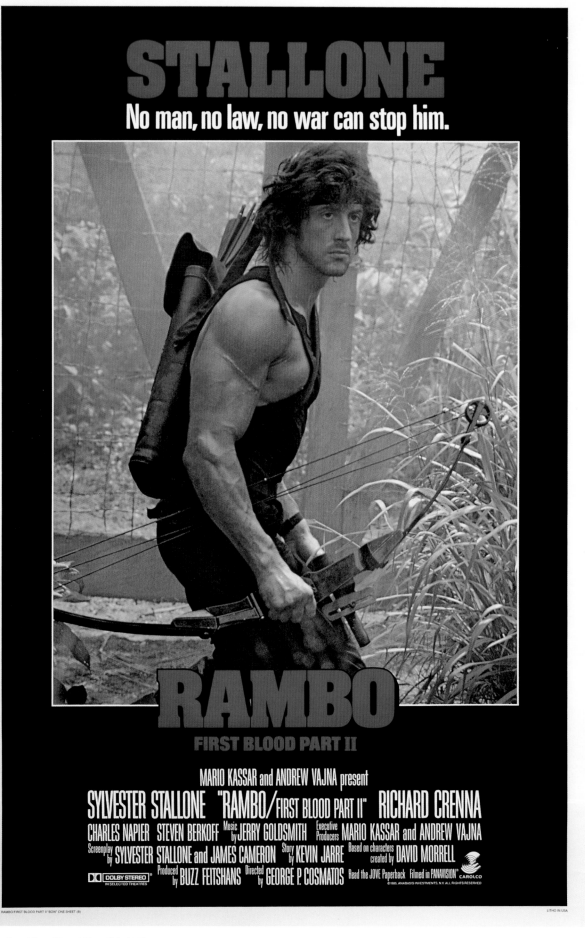

**Rambo: First Blood Part II** (1985)
US 41 × 27 in. (104 × 69 cm)
('Bow' Style B)

**First Blood** (1982)
US 41 × 27 in. (104 × 69 cm)
Art direction & design by Bill Pate
Illustration by Drew Struzan

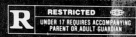

Raiders Of The Lost Ark
(1981)
US 41 × 27 in. (104 × 69 cm)
Art by Richard Amsel

**Raiders Of The Lost Ark** (1981)
Polish 38 × 26 in. (97 × 66 cm)
Art by Jakub Erol

# Indiana Jones—the new hero from the creators of JAWS and STAR WARS.

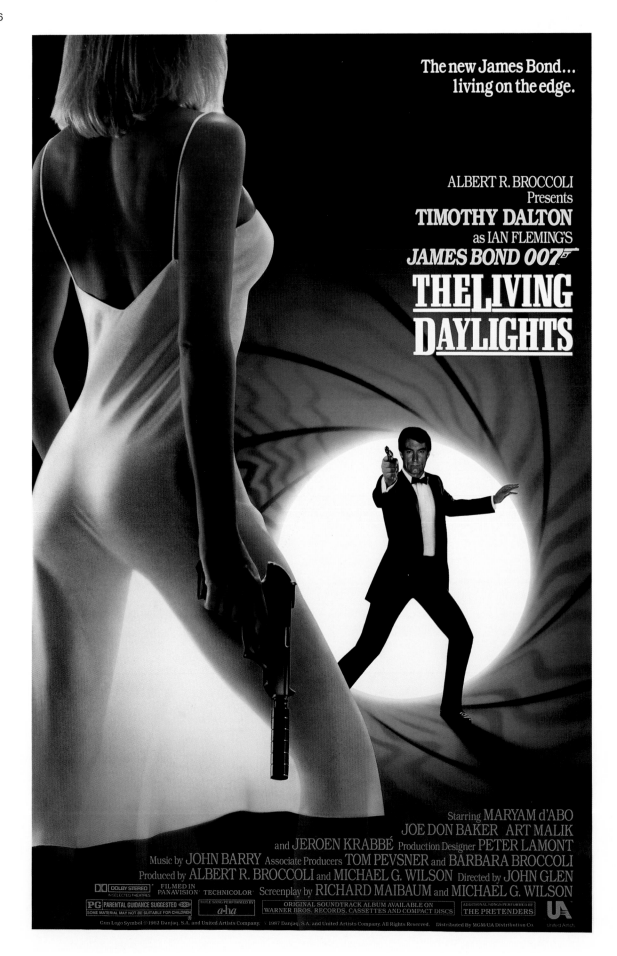

**The Living Daylights** (1987)
US 41 × 27 in. (104 × 69 cm)
Art direction & design by Jeffrey Bacon & David Reneric
Photo by Jim McCrary

**A View To A Kill** (1985)
British 41 × 27 in. (104 × 69 cm)
Art by Vic Fair

# Has JAMES BOND met his match?

The Right Stuff (1983)
US 41 × 27 in. (104 × 69 cm)
(Advance)

Top Gun (1986)
US 41 × 27 in. (104 × 69 cm)

# THE RIGHT STUFF

## How the future began.

A ROBERT CHARTOFF-IRWIN WINKLER Production of A PHILIP KAUFMAN Film "THE RIGHT STUFF"
CHARLES FRANK · SCOTT GLENN · ED HARRIS · LANCE HENRIKSEN · SCOTT PAULIN · DENNIS QUAID
SAM SHEPARD · FRED WARD · KIM STANLEY · BARBARA HERSHEY · VERONICA CARTWRIGHT
PAMELA REED   Music by BILL CONTI   Director of Photography CALEB DESCHANEL   Based on the Book by TOM WOLFE
Produced by IRWIN WINKLER and ROBERT CHARTOFF   Written for the Screen and Directed by PHILIP KAUFMAN

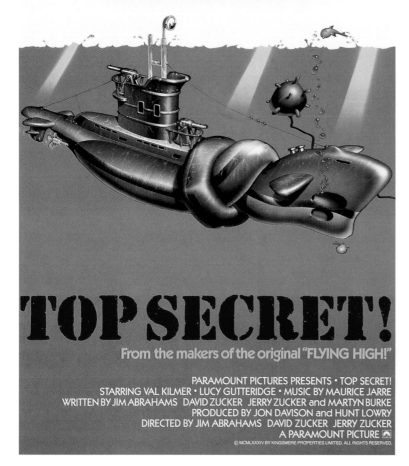

**Top Secret** (1984)
British 41 × 27 in. (104 × 69 cm)
(Style A)

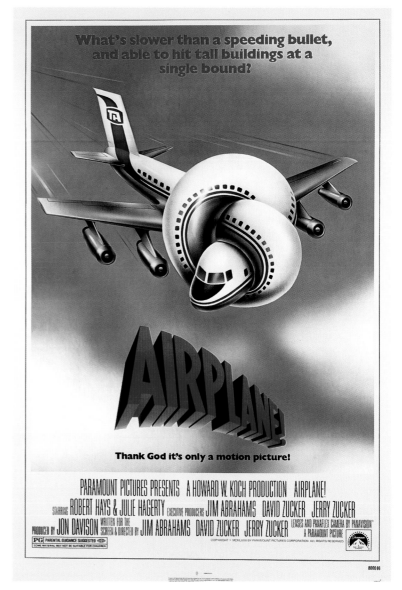

**Airplane!** (1980)
US 41 × 27 in. (104 × 69 cm)

**Naked Gun:**
**From The Files Of Police Squad!** (1988)
US 41 × 27 in. (104 × 69 cm)
Art direction & design by John McTague
Photo by Joe Mineau & Steve Schapiro

**Ferris Bueller's Day Off** (1986)
British 41 × 27 in. (104 × 69 cm)
Art by A. Purkis

**Back To The Future** (1985)
US 41 × 27 in. (104 × 69 cm)
Art by Drew Struzan

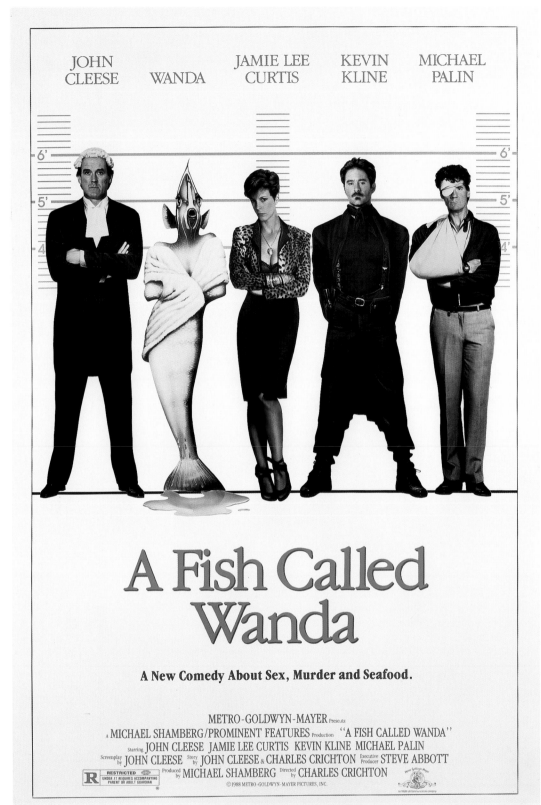

**A Fish Called Wanda** (1988)
US 41 × 27 in. (104 × 69 cm)

**Tootsie** (1982)
US 41 × 27 in. (104 × 69 cm)
(Advance)

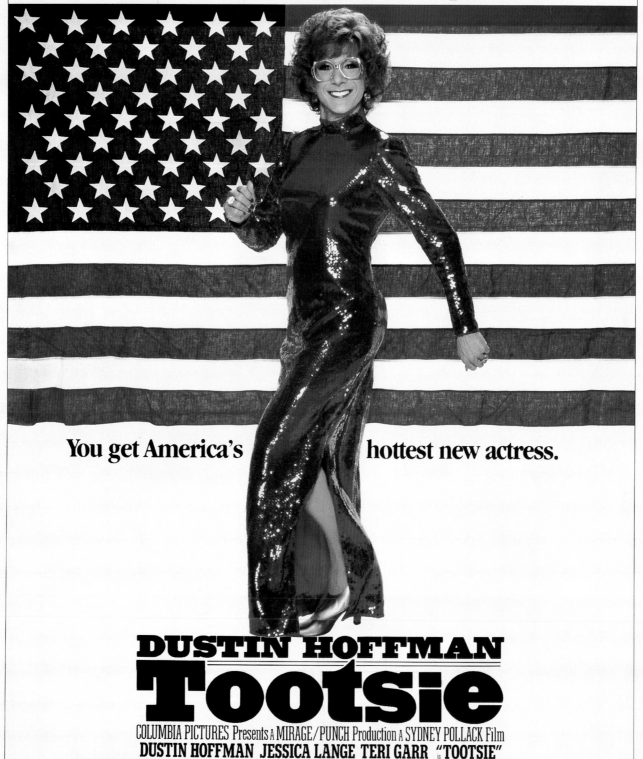

What do you get when you cross a hopelessly straight, starving actor with a dynamite red sequined dress?

You get America's hottest new actress.

# DUSTIN HOFFMAN
# Tootsie

COLUMBIA PICTURES Presents A MIRAGE/PUNCH Production A SYDNEY POLLACK Film

**DUSTIN HOFFMAN JESSICA LANGE TERI GARR** in "TOOTSIE"

DABNEY COLEMAN CHARLES DURNING Music by DAVE GRUSIN Original/Lyrics by ALAN & MARILYN BERGMAN Songs/Music by DAVE GRUSIN Song by STEPHEN BISHOP Executive Producer CHARLES EVANS

Story by DON McGUIRE and LARRY GELBART Screenplay by LARRY GELBART and MURRAY SCHISGAL Produced by SYDNEY POLLACK and DICK RICHARDS

**PG** PARENTAL GUIDANCE SUGGESTED
SOME MATERIAL MAY NOT BE SUITABLE FOR CHILDREN

Directed by SYDNEY POLLACK

© 1982 COLUMBIA PICTURES INDUSTRIES, INC.

This Christmas everyone will know
that she's Dustin Hoffman and he's Tootsie.

**Fletch** (1985)
US 41 × 27 in. (104 × 69 cm)
(Advance)

**Ghostbusters** (1984)
US 41 × 27 in. (104 × 69 cm)
Art direction by Steve Kasloff & Kevin Nolan
Design by Michael Gross

*"They're here."*

# POLTERGEIST

*It knows what scares you.*

METRO-GOLDWYN-MAYER Presents

A STEVEN SPIELBERG Production

A TOBE HOOPER Film "POLTERGEIST" JOBETH WILLIAMS · CRAIG T. NELSON · BEATRICE STRAIGHT   Music by JERRY GOLDSMITH
Special Visual Effects by INDUSTRIAL LIGHT & MAGIC A Division of Lucasfilm Ltd.   Story by STEVEN SPIELBERG   Screenplay by STEVEN SPIELBERG, MICHAEL GRAIS & MARK VICTOR
Directed by TOBE HOOPER   Produced by STEVEN SPIELBERG and FRANK MARSHALL   METROCOLOR   Released thru MGM/UA Entertainment Co.

Soundtrack Album available on MGM Records & Tapes
Manufactured and marketed by PolyGram Records

READ THE WARNER BOOK

 DOLBY STEREO ™
IN SELECTED THEATRES

© 1982 Metro-Goldwyn-Mayer Film Co. and SLM Entertainment Ltd.

**The Untouchables** (1987)
US 41 × 27 in. (104 × 69 cm)
Art direction by Tony Seiniger
Design by Tony Seiniger, Olga Kaljakin & Dan Chapman
Photo by Richard Nobel

**Scarface** (1983)
US 41 × 27 in. (104 × 69 cm)

# AL PACINO SCARFACE

In the spring of 1980, the port at Mariel Harbor was opened, and thousands set sail for the United States. They came in search of the American Dream.

One of them found it on the sun-washed avenues of Miami…wealth, power and passion beyond his wildest dreams.

He was Tony Montana. The world will remember him by another name …SCARFACE.

He loved the American Dream. With a vengeance.

A MARTIN BREGMAN PRODUCTION

A BRIAN De PALMA FILM

AL PACINO "SCARFACE"

SCREENPLAY BY OLIVER STONE

MUSIC BY GIORGIO MORODER

DIRECTOR OF PHOTOGRAPHY JOHN A. ALONZO A.S.C.

EXECUTIVE PRODUCER LOUIS A. STROLLER

PRODUCED BY MARTIN BREGMAN

DIRECTED BY BRIAN De PALMA

SOUNDTRACK AVAILABLE ON MCA RECORDS AND CASSETTES.
A UNIVERSAL PICTURE/READ THE BERKLEY BOOK.

830167
SCARFACE

**Once Upon A Time In America** (1984)
German 33 × 46 in. (84 × 117 cm)
Art by Renato Casaro

**Once Upon A Time In America** (1984)
Hungarian 31 × 23 in. (79 × 58 cm)
Art by F. Molnar

**Raging Bull** (1980)
US 41 × 27 in. (104 × 69 cm)
(First Advance)
Art direction by Larry Lurin
Design by Merv Block & Larry Lurin
Illustration by Kunio Hagio

**Raging Bull** (1980)
Czech 33 × 23 in. (84 × 58 cm)
Art direction & Illustration by Zdenek Ziegler

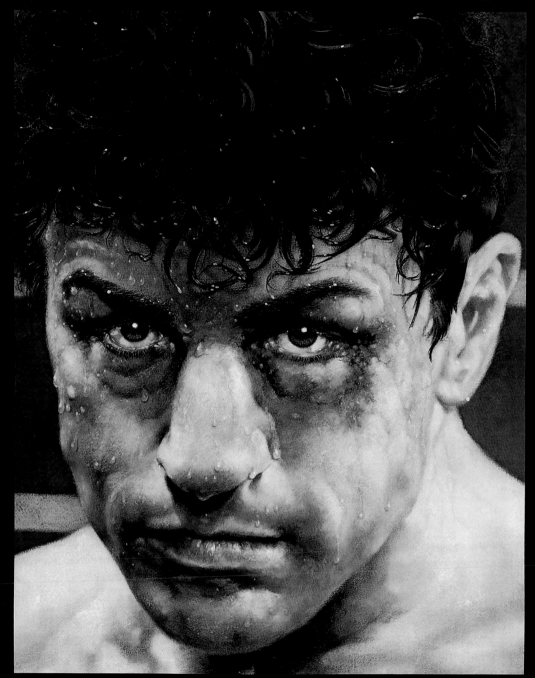

DE NIRO

RAGING

**United Artists**
A Transamerica Company

"RAGING BULL"

126

# index of film titles

Title Page:
**Commando** (1985)
US 41 × 27 in. (104 × 69 cm)
Art direction by Tony Seiniger
Design by Tracy Western
Photo by Bruce McBroom

Back Cover:
**The Blues Brothers** (1980)
US 41 × 27 in. (104 × 69 cm)

**Reds** (1981)
US 41 × 27 in. (104 × 69 cm)
(Advance)

# ALSO AVAILABLE

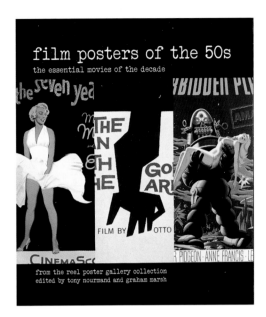

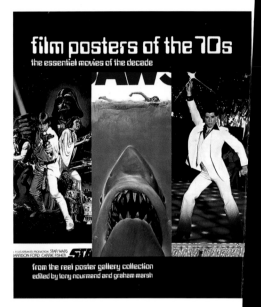

**Film posters of the 50s** gives a stimulating insight into movie making of the era.
**DESIGN WEEK**

From *Some Like It Hot* to *Forbidden Planet*, Tony Nourmand and Graham Marsh amass a staggering trove of film posters of the 50s.
**VANITY FAIR**

The wretchedly dull Eisenhower Fifties had plenty popping on the big screen. Nobody smoked a cigarette like James Dean. Nobody stood on a subway grate like Marilyn Monroe. **Film posters of the 50s**, by Tony Nourmand and Graham Marsh, documents when movies were epic and stars were fabulous.

**PLAYBOY**

**Film posters of the 60s** evokes an era when James Bond flicks were envelope-pushing fantasies for the bachelor-pad set.
**NEWSWEEK**

Here is a book which, for once, delivers just what you would expect from the title … For poster collectors – and everyone else – this is a crisp and stylish picture book.
**DAILY MAIL**

No commentary needed for this high-quali catalogue of the most evocative poster art of t decade taste forgot.
**SIGHT AND SOUND**

Film books naturally lend themselves to images a a really well-designed book of film poster art c prove contagiously entertaining and informative only to discover how differently movies are market in other countries. **Film posters of the 70s** does j what it says on the cover.

**EVENING STANDARD**

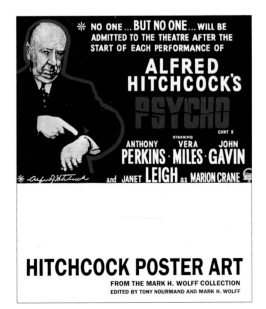

A magnificent celebration of both Hitchcock and the Cinema itself.
**TOTAL FILM**

Any film fan worth his or her salt will shoot off to the local bookshop and immediately purchase this superb book…. Utterly brilliant.

**FILM REVIEW**